Women Speak

Volume Eight

Edited by Kari Gunter-Seymour

Story ~ Poetry ~ Song
Fine Art

Women Speak Volume Eight © 2022 Women of Appalachia Project
A 501(C)(3) non-profit organization

ISBN: 9798985524291
Sheila-Na-Gig Editions
Russell, KY
www.sheilanagigblog.com

EDITOR: Kari Gunter-Seymour
LINE EDITOR: Kristine Williams
COVER DESIGN: Kari Gunter-Seymour
COVER ART: *Babies,* Diana Ferguson

INQUIRIES:
Kari Gunter-Seymour, Executive Director
womenofappalachia@gmail.com
www.womenofappalachia.com
FACEBOOK: Women of Appalachia Project

Women Speak

Volume Eight

Contents:

INTRODUCTION:

FINE ART:

Introduction

Dear Reader,

When I am asked to describe the Women of Appalachia Project, I say this: WOAP is an arts organization comprised of an extraordinary group of women with strong Appalachian roots, working to empower ourselves and other female writers and artists, as well as our communities, through live and published presentations of story, poetry, song, and visual art.

Today I was reminded that it has been barely 100 years since women won the right to vote in our country, and when I say "women" I have to clarify "white women." It took another forty-five years to win that right for women of color, a shameful fact. It is no secret that we are undervalued, paid less, provided fewer opportunities for advancement and of late, as if it were once again the dark ages, we have been stripped of authority over our own bodies.

Women from Appalachia keenly understand the concept of being considered "less than," having been looked down upon for generations. We have learned by experience that, as women, we must work together to achieve our goals if we are to survive and thrive. WOAP encourages Appalachian-based female voices to rise up and speak their truths, or slap it down on a piece of paper, frame it, and hang it out in the sun for all to see. We do so with abundant respect for one another, our culture, and this land we so highly value.

No need for marches or protest signs; our work speaks for itself. We are: A PRINDI Award winner, Weatherford Award winners, state and municipal Poet Laureates, Pushcart Prize and Best of the Net awardees and nominees, and authors of acclaimed books. We are all shapes and sizes. Some of us are differently-abled, some are in recovery, some work two jobs, care for kids or ailing parents, and still somehow manage to create and contribute. Many of us come from ancestries full of remarkable women who worked the fields, then the factories or retail (some still do) children on their hips or strapped to their backs, scrappers every one. From this we draw our strength, endurance, and determination to pay it forward to our own and future generations. We are aware of what's at stake and that we must stay the course.

And just to be clear, reader, we will not back down.

> "Mid-stem an ancient-green leaf is curled like
> a hand on the hip—daring and sassy." —Sheila Carter-Jones

Kari Gunter-Seymour
Founder/Executive Director
Women of Appalachia Project

E. J. Wade

Collateral

later when time has passed
and the marrow of her bones
has returned to mix itself with
the earth -   remnants
of her-story   rescued from
yellow spotted hat boxes and leathered
trunks   rusted and
decayed from age and disregard

her voice pieced together and resurrected
like the passage of
ancestors shackled, scattered and

sold at market value
by those who knew her only by
the facility of her body

bought and sold
from cradle to grave
a commodity   valued
and   priced pound per pound
        of rendered muscle and flesh
used as collateral
long after her body
relinquished its spirit
at the jumping off point
we will remember

E. J. Wade

Lineage

I watched her fingers crooked with age
part her hair from years of practice

intertwining the strands like sisal
over and under and over again
plaiting a braid that like an anchor
rests at the base of her back

Black as the coal that took my
grandfather to an early grave
her hair is proof, reminder that the
roots of our lineage lay in the strands
of the DNA of generations
long erased from his-story and hers

Stroking her hair with my nimble fingers
I place a kiss ever so gently atop her head
in tribute of our unbreakable bond

Resting my face in the crick of her neck
I pay homage in knowing that
not even death can separate us

E. J. Wade

Mama Makes Music

mama makes music
every time she beats
air into the whites of eggs

whisking faster than
the speed of light
mountains and peaks
rise high and voluminous
crowning glorious meringue
toasted brown and singing
praise and glory

mama makes music
every time she scrubs the collars
and cuffs of daddy's work
shirt and tattered pants
rub-a-dub against the galvanized
wash board handed down from
her mother and then to her

mama makes music
every time she rocks
away my hurt and pain
with the gentle patting
of her hand against my back
and the tapping of her feet
anchored in the hallowed
spirituals of captivity and struggle
My mama makes music

Susan Sheppard

How My Father Babysat

I remember the Camel cigarette pinched
Between my father's nicotine fingers, his
Plum red face, cheekbones that could cut glass.
Dad would steady me over the car's console
And together we would travel the backroads
Searching out liquor stores and unshaven Indian graves.
Afterwards, rain puddles spat mud against the side
Of our white jeep. Then we'd stop at every
Mom and Pop beer joint in the wood tick
Thickets beyond town as an overhead fan
Whipped over us with fly paper strung
Like yellow guts against the ceiling.
Outside the jumping juke joint, the grey boards
Separated like the gaps in the teeth of a bum.
The drunks would put a quarter in the juke box
So I could do my savage dance
As Dad laughed through crackling lungs.
Together we could outrun anything . . . black bears,
Bill collectors, mad hornets, the sheriff and my mother.
From my father I learned not to be on anyone's side,
That Shawnee know to run, we already know how to hide.

Susan Sheppard

To Be Indian

You must adjust yourself to what is,
Like bones dug up from the clay, arranged in a drawer
Only to be shelved. To be Indian is to be ghosted
By other lives, to sense the world
Through your hair, to have it flow
In long bolts and never cut
The dark oil that springs
From your scalp left to
Spill over a red moon face.
To be Indian is to know that skins
Are sometimes for wearing,
To know everything that matters is red,
Even a small bead dropped on the ground.
To be Indian is to be frightened
By the sudden knocking on doors
And the unexpected ringing of phones
Yet to know it is not dangerous
To dance in a fire
And bleed maroon
Over a bean-brown nipple.
To be Indian is to slink into corners
Unseen, to know you are the only
Dirty animal perspiring in the room.
To be Indian is to know that as long
As you don't move, no one will realize that
You are even there. To be Indian is to remain still,
And know that invisible things will call to you,
Distantly, and for a long time.

Ellis Elliott

Counting Backwards

(Martha)

I lie still in bed, counting backwards
in time with the lift and lower of my chest
slowing my shivers. I listen and wait
for Daniel's high-pitched trill, his signal
no rebels in sight, he's made his break
away from our home and back to his men, again.

I sawed the circle of trapdoor underneath, wide
enough for him to slip through for time beside me.
My skin smells of horse and sweat and I taste
his grime on my lips. My thin nightgown
is damp with him.

The lock is latched between his world
and mine. I count the days since my blood
last flowed, hold my stretched belly and pray
to fallow fields on an old moon, please no more.

I count the days until she comes, cob pipe
between her lips, river branches etched
above and below. Granny Grills will bring
skullcap for Sis's black moods, primrose
and a plug of tobacco for mine.

I listen for Daniel's high-pitched trill, his signal
he's made his break away from our bed
and I am alone, again.

Ellis Elliott

Widow Campbell

(Granny Grills)

She said the blue flame swung like his lantern used to,
from barn to house, long after he died. Some said
it was her consumption talking, but I know it's true.

Spirits know who needs visiting, and they know who
to avoid. She'd place his empty boots at guard by the door.
She said the blue flame swung like his lantern used to,

and stopped still at the end of her bed. She felt his warmth
calm the shiver in her bones. Eppie Peck swears she saw him
walking from barn to house, long after he died. Some say

they saw Eppie whispering by the creek bank to the wind. Widow
Campbell cleaned wet mud from his boot treads, although some said
it was her consumption talking. I know the truth.

Ellis Elliott

Eppie

(Sis)

Her hair as black as mine, she was hunting rabbits
behind our house when I first laid eyes on her.
She darted in and out of the stand of white pines
like playing hide-and-seek, and I finally gathered
my skirt to run near and yell a greeting. She shied
away like a shot deer at first, until I waved and smiled.
A half-raised hand hello back to me, and her eyes
as wide as a blinking owl, we learned each other
in the woods that day. Her skin even darker than mine,
we became friends when we could find time after
chores, climbing trees easy as squirrels and talking.
I don't know what it was that she left unsaid, but
it grew thick around us like tree shadows at dusk.

I know this. Once here, she didn't ever want to leave our house.
She'd wait for the last ribbon of sun on the ridge before setting out.

Kathy Guest
Inside Thoughts

Karen Spears Zacharias

Demon Child

INTRODUCTION

The Supreme Court is not infallible. Sometimes they make rulings that are wickedly wrong. Such was the case in May 1927, when United States Supreme Court Chief Justice Oliver Wendell Holmes wrote a decision that empowered states to forcibly sterilize men and women. As a result of that case, *Buck v. Bell*, Carrie Buck, 21, was sterilized in October of that same year. The US would go on to sterilize an estimated 70,000 people (Cohen, 2016). Deemed "manifestly unfit" to parent, Carrie was labeled "feebleminded" and sterilized by the State of Virginia five months following the 8-1 Supreme Court decision. In the decision targeting Carrie Buck, Justice Holmes wrote: "Three generations of imbeciles are enough" (Lombardo, 2008).

Justice Holmes failed to consider that a lack of education does not equate to being feebleminded any more than being educated ensures that one is wise. Carrie was entrapped in a system that rendered her *undereducated,* and then imprisoned her for the education she was denied. At the time of the Supreme Court ruling, Carrie and her mother were incarcerated at the Virginia Colony for Epileptics and the Feebleminded.

Compulsory sterilization, as granted under *Buck v. Bell*, remains law to this day. Although it is reported that Oregon (the state I live in) was the last to legally practice compulsory sterilization, there have been troubling accounts that some who do not understand the legal system, or their rights within that system, continue to be wrongly sterilized. In 2017, Tennessee Judge Sam Benningfield was reprimanded for offering defendants less jail time if they would agree to a vasectomy (Tamburin, 2019). In 2020, Dawn Wooten, a nurse at the Irwin County Detention Center in Ocilla, Georgia, filed a whistleblower's complaint regarding the sterilization of undocumented immigrants. Following Wooten's complaint, sixteen Irwin County detainees came forward to say they suffered from invasive gynecological medical surgeries and exams, including forced sterilizations (Harman, 2021). These detainees reported being punished for speaking out, some of whom were then deported, and Wooten lost her job because of her whistleblower complaint.

It was while reading an article about the latter incident that I began to learn about the history of compulsory sterilization in America. I was deeply disturbed by the account of sisters Minne Lee and Mary Alice Relf, who were sterilized in 1973 at the ages of 12 and 14 in Montgomery, Alabama, solely because they were black and from a poor family (Taylor,

2021). Eventually, I traced their situation back to the story of Carrie Buck and our nation's shameful devotion to Eugenics, the belief that there are "inheritable traits" that can form a superior race, and that race is white.

I read numerous books about Carrie's court case including Paul A. Lombardo's *Three Generations, No Imbeciles* (Lombardo, 2008). Lombardo was a young law student when he became interested in the wrongs done to Carrie. Today, he is considered the preeminent scholar on Carrie Buck. While others have studied Carrie Buck, many accept the narrative of the court, referring to Buck as "slow" or "mentally disabled." Some have resorted to the archaic "imbecile" or "feebleminded" narrative. It was Lombardo who chased down Carrie's school records, and later, her hand-written letters, proving that Carrie Buck was quite capable of learning, and was, in fact, literate.

At age 17, Carrie became pregnant, delivered a daughter, and was then incarcerated to the Virginia Colony for Epileptics and the Feebleminded. Lombardo, who interviewed Carrie weeks before her death, disputes the court's assertion that Carrie was sexually promiscuous. Lombardo documented Carrie's account that she was raped. Lombardo noted that it was the rapist's aunt and uncle—Carrie's foster parents—who had Carrie committed to the eugenics colony. Once she was committed, they claimed custody of her infant daughter. Carrie's rapist suffered no legal consequences for his crime. Carrie, however, was confined to the eugenics colony until she was 21, and she lived with the fear of being sent back to the colony for years to come. It was during her confinement that the sterilization case was brought before the Supreme Court. Five months following the 8-1 decision in favor of compulsory sterilization, Carrie underwent the knife.

Carrie was a girl robbed of her mother, who grew to be a woman robbed of her daughter, and a mother robbed of the right to bear more children. What did she do with all the grief and pain of all those losses? How did she find the wherewithal to carry on? What was Carrie thinking and feeling as men made decisions about her life? Her daughter's life? Her mother's life? Who were the helpers in Carrie's life? Did she have anyone to turn to when she was raped? Where is Carrie's voice in all the stories told about her?

At this time in history, when women's reproductive rights are once again under attack by the courts, by men and women seeking to determine who should reproduce and when, Carrie's story resonates powerfully. Lacking a diary, or her own writings on the matter, we can only imagine her struggles and how she coped. So that is what I have done in the following pages—created an imaginary account of Carrie's life, while drawing from the various books written about Carrie and the court case, the handful of letters that Carrie penned, the brief interviews she granted late in life, and the various newspaper and magazine articles written about Carrie's plight.

I've relied on research where it was available and where it is not, I turned to my imagination. There was a time when I, too, like Carrie was 17 and pregnant. I remember what a frightening and confusing time of life that was for me. It is from that well that I attempt to resurrect Carrie's voice for present and future generations to hear. Denied the opportunity to speak for herself in life, I hope that this work will amplify her voice now.

DEMON CHILD

J. T. couldn't afford for locals to think the girl child was being mistreated, even though he agreed with Alice—the child was marred. Carrie was dumb as a donkey and twice as stubborn. Maybe if she had been born a boy, her feeble mind might not have mattered much. A boy with brute strength could be a useful thing to have around. Who cared if a boy could speak as long as he could load and unload a wagon when ordered to? But a mute girl was a quare thing. J.T. Dobbs had it in mind that Carrie might very well be some sort of demonic spook sent to punish him. He wished he'd known all that before he and the missus agreed to take the girl in.

Here he was thinking all that time he was doing the Christian thing when it may very well have been a pre-ordained thing all along. Some days J.T. wondered if God was mocking him, setting him up on account of the things he did with the girl's momma, Emma. Alice didn't know about any of those things, and it was J.T.'s intention that she'd go to her grave never knowing. He'd fell out of love with Alice years ago, shortly after their daughter Effie died. He hadn't meant to quit loving her. Does anybody ever intend such a thing?

He'd fallen hard for her at first. A cousin introduced the two of them downtown one Saturday afternoon. Alice was on her way to meet her mom, and J.T. was finishing up a lunch break. She was smartly dressed in a navy frock cinched tightly, highlighting her taut waist and ample bosom. She had on matching gloves and button-up boots. Her auburn hair was pinned up so that natural curls fell around the crown of her head in a sassy fashion, like a hat askew. But what really captured J.T. were her eyes. They were the blue of a morning sky in May, piercingly brilliant. He could not quit staring at her even though he knew it was forward of him. She was only 17 and he was practically middle-aged at 33.

If only Alice had stayed that girl, perhaps J.T. could love her as he did then. But Effie's death had changed her. It had changed J.T., too, but it was easier to blame Alice for all that went wrong than to admit to any wrongdoing on his part. It was nearly a year after Effie's death before

22

Alice welcomed J.T. back into her bed, into her arms. Alice may have suspected, but J.T. never confirmed that he'd been seeking his pleasures elsewhere. He told himself he was doing her a favor, letting her cry herself to sleep, letting her wallow in her grief. For 23 days, Effie had been the center of their world. When she died, inexplicably, their world fell apart. They would go on to live as husband and wife, go on to have other children, even go on to lose other children, but nothing was ever the same again after Effie's death. That unvarnished hope in all things good that the young seem to possess was gone.

Looking at her now, sitting in the porch swing, J.T. wished he felt nothing towards her. Feeling nothing would be preferable to loathing her, which, if he were being honest with himself, he did. Alice manifested all the disappointments of their life together. Ever since they'd taken in Emma's girl, Alice was in a perpetual state of mad. He'd come home from work early and found Carrie tied to a tree in the backyard, wearing nothing but her panties. Fire ants crawled up her legs, leaving welts in their wake. The ten-year-old had peed on herself but she wasn't wailing. Her chin rested on her naked chest, and she was weeping ever so softly.

"What the hell is going on?" J.T. asked as he stormed into the house, after first untying the child.

From where she was at the kitchen table, Alice could see J.T. a'coming, but she went right on wiping down the jars of peaches she'd been canning that afternoon. She didn't even look up when the screen door slammed behind him. Carrie stayed on the other side of the door, standing on the stoop, unsure of what she was supposed to do now.

"I asked you a question: What is going on here?" J.T. hollered again. His neck was flushed. Sweat beaded on his forehead. He wanted to snatch Alice up by her hair and knock some sense into her, but he restrained himself. He was keenly aware there was a child standing beyond the door watching him.

Without even so much as a glance his way, Alice responded, "She was misbehaving." Alice turned her back to J.T. and folded the damp rag over the cupboard door to dry.

"Misbehaving? What could Carrie have done that would cause you to tie her up to a tree like a yard dog?"

"Don't be coming in here yelling at me," Alice retorted. Turning to face J.T. now, she tore into him, "You are the one who brought that demon child into this house. I never wanted her here in the first place. Something is wrong with that child. No wonder her momma gave her away!"

J.T. looked back over his shoulder at Carrie. It was clear she was terrified to say or do anything, but she wasn't crying anymore. She was still as stone. J.T. got right up in Alice's face, almost nose to nose, and through gritted teeth, demanded of her: "What is wrong with you, woman?

Speaking about a child in front of her like that? She's a child for Christ's sake, but she knows exactly what you are saying!"

"I don't give a shit!" Alice spit out the words. "She's not my child. She's some whore's child!"

J.T. hauled off and slapped Alice across the face. He couldn't help it. What she said about Emma was uncalled for, and he couldn't tolerate anybody saying such hateful things about a child. No child should ever be told they are unwanted. Children can't help the circumstances to which they are born. They don't pick their parents.

Alice's hand went to her face, and she bolted from the kitchen, "You are going to burn in hell for this, J.T.!"

J.T. figured she might be right about that, and so much more, but at that moment he didn't really care much about eternal damnation. Opening the screen door, he took Carrie by the hand and sat her on the kitchen counter. Taking a clean rag from the drawer, he washed Carrie's face, then her hands, and lastly, and more gently, he washed her legs which were eat up with fire ant bites. Slicing up a cucumber he placed the coolness against the bites.

"How's that feel?" he asked. "Better?"

Carrie looked up through her thick lashes and nodded.

After some of the redness went away, J.T. dabbed the bites with honey. "Have you had anything to drink?"

Carrie shook her head.

He handed her a dipper of water. She drank it all down, hurriedly, then handed it back to him. Once he was sure Carrie was hydrated, and her legs tended to, J.T. cut up a peach and fed the child. He guessed from the way Carrie devoured the peach, skin, and all that she hadn't eaten all day. At least not since breakfast. He noticed the rope burns on her belly and around her wrist.

Then it occurred to J.T. that Alice had never said what Carrie had done that prompted her to tie the child to a tree in the first place. J.T. figured it didn't really matter: What could Alice possibly tell him that would have justified what she'd done to that poor child? One thing was clear though, Alice had set a course for the child that would lead to destruction—either theirs or the child's. Maybe both.

Works Cited

Cohen, Adam, and Terry Gross. "The Supreme Court Ruling That Led to 70,000 Forced Sterilizations." *Fresh Air*, National Public Radio. 7 March 2016.

Harman, Andrew. "One Year after Dawn Wooten's Disclosures of Immigrant Abuse, Irwin County Detention Center Finally Moves out All Detained Immigrants." Government Accountability Project. 9 Sept. 2021.

Lombardo, Paul A. *Three Generations, No Imbeciles*. Baltimore: Johns Hopkins University Press, 2008.

Tamburin, Adam. "Court Revives Lawsuit against Judge Who Shortened Jail Time If Inmates Got Sterilized." *The Tennessean*, 4 Apr. 2019.

Taylor, Mildred Europa. "48 Years Ago, Minnie and Her Mentally Disabled Sister Were Sterilized without Their Knowledge, Sparking Lawsuit and Change." *Face2Face Africa*. 12 Feb. 2021.

Note: Demon Child is a chapter in the forthcoming book, *A Soul to Save* (Mercer Univ. Press)

Sam Campbell

Rural Legend No. 14: Willow Woman

On melancholy nights shrouded in fog, she wails;
a poor peasant girl turned weeping willow.
Combing riverbank corpses among the cattails
and, failing, her sorrow she'll bellow.

A poor peasant girl turned weeping willow;
she sought love from the hearts of males
and, failing, her sorrow she'll bellow,
growing, ballooning amongst her entrails.

She sought love from the hearts of males;
he gave instead a baby, soon to show,
growing, ballooning amongst her entrails.
Future so bleak, the child's life she'd forego.

He gave instead a baby, soon to show.
Once born the babe cries, hiccups, flails.
Future so bleak, the child's life she'd forego;
plunged deep, stolen screams, life stales.

Once born the babe cries, hiccups, flails.
Combing riverbank corpses among the cattails—
plunged deep, stolen screams, life stales—
on melancholy nights shrouded in fog, she wails.

Kari Gunter-Seymour

Mysterious Ways

Nine weeks, no monthlies,
my body a nestling's perch,
a tremoring tree, leaning

into a southeaster, hard luck
and poverty licking red-hot
flames against my bent back.

I scrimped, saved, still forty dollars
short of the cash I'd need to set
me and that little bird free.

No stranger to a bowed head,
I got straight to the appeal, laid out
my endgame and trading points.

The Lord coughed up two twenties
by way of a birthday card, sent postage due
from my granny, who wrote at length

about her late-night vision. She saw
me old, alone in the dark,
crying out for some little bird.

Kari Gunter-Seymour

It Isn't Ever Delicate to Live

She feels like last night's wine bottle,
nothing left inside but grainy, bitter bits.
In a magazine at the Vet's Office,
she read women over fifty obsess
about mortality. These days, she thinks
less about her death, than of living too long,
impoverished, her life a footnote
in the Baptist church bulletin.
A woman who rarely cries though
she might be better for it, awake night
after night, imagining a life, brittle bones
jutting her calico fleece. No wonder
she's talking to the air, walking
the deer track home alone, jaw clenched,
a worn leash and empty collar
clutched dearly to her chest.

Kari Gunter-Seymour

Land Lessons

She's lived here all her life,
a gift to know this land, its seasons,
tastes, smells, mindful of its wants—
even knowing every acre was once taken
by violence. We all have mortifications,
history's footprints threaded among the trees.

From the porch, sunset paints the surface
of the pond, pregnant with twigs
and twitchy insects, a Gaia of breeze
strums shuffled reeds.
She's had a good cry, one that could
have left a lesser woman sharp-cornered.

Later she will wash the dishes,
her face splashed and wakened,
remind herself how the heat
of evening warms the bones.

She was alone when she entered this world,
she'll be alone when she leaves it,
her life unremarkable as the house fly
balanced on her dinner plate,
rubbing its bristly bowed legs together.

S. Renay Sanders

In the Shadow

Punxsutawney shadowing
Deep, sometimes wide
Across the landscape
Ground hog day
Spectacle
Six more weeks
Or not

Hiding underlying wisdom
Of ancient ones
Who have long predicted
The coming of spring
Earth's quickening
Felt by all
Crones, witches, and hags

Called by Brighid to the
Circle of wisdom
Luna dance in the starlight
Wind swept crispness
Contrasting bonfire's blaze

Imbolc prediction of
Winter days remaining
More logs for the fire
Or seeds tucked into
Beds of loam?
This is Brighid's story
Of long ago,
Still available
to the sages

All else distracted
By the joke, the laugh
The spectacle
Ground hogging
Keeping women's wisdom
In the shadows

Marianne Worthington

Reprise

The roof sips the rain
and spits it out again.
The downspout
clatters a downbeat
of uneven accents
before pouring
a cradle of rainwater
in the yard. Newly
uncradled rabbits leap
and sink in the wet
ruins of the understory
not yet greening. Spring
is overdue and has cried
about it all month, bringing
a sorrow to the sky,
repeating the violet
bruise on the world you
would only see if you're
the hawk on the scoop
for a song sparrow.

Marianne Worthington

Mildred Falls as Dominant 7ᵗʰ Chord

Her musical instincts were brighter than stained-glass
windows on a Sunday morning, but she was forgotten
quick as a trill, an ornament lost in the praise song

of Mahalia Jackson. The Broadway musical
about Mahalia didn't bother to mention Mildred,
discarded she was, like an old hymnbook

with a broken spine. While still a child, she heard
Mahalia sing in a Chicago church, announced
her intentions to learn piano, and even though

she went to conservatory and studied theory,
composition, harmony, her secret to buoyant playing
was to lead with her bosom, power that force down

her arms, to her poised wrists, out to her fingers
that stroked like pistons. You couldn't have
a delicate left hand with Mahalia. Honey,

you had to match that fire with power chords
grown deep in the garden of the church, nurtured
in preacher songs, flowering in swaying choirs.

Pretty soon crowds wanted *her* autograph too,
a signature as pretty as her arpeggios—
"Mildred Falls, pianist"—her letters looping

like the inverted dominant 7ᵗʰ chords she riffed
to fill the spaces in Mahalia's impulsive habits:
no rehearsing, changing the tempo mid-song,

breathing in the most absurd spaces. Part jazz,
part holler, all gospel and ring shout, Mildred led
the way for other players—Aretha, Billy, Leon—

but she made no money, $100 a week for over 20 years.
When she asked for more, Mahalia fired her on the spot
never thinking what folks remember when they recall

Didn't It Rain or *Elijah Rock* or *How I Got Over*.
It's the thunder of Mildred's fingers flooding dark
blues, agony and woe, how her piano playing shook

the halls and sanctuaries and studios, how the notes
lifted her above Mahalia's yoke, how that piano
echoes the hallelujah we didn't even know we needed.

Marianne Worthington

Morning walk haibun

Our yards are full of political signs ahead of the upcoming elections, and I don't really like knowing who my neighbors support for office. I prefer to judge them on the remarkable things I've seen in their yards: a Fifth-Wheel hulking by the ditch, the red pickup parked in a side yard for two decades, vines choking the undercarriage, the juniper border littered with eggshells, the fence rows, like mine, creeping with yellow rocket and morning glories. I like living among the detritus of rural people. I grew up on concrete playgrounds. The sidewalks in my grandmother's neighborhood buckled and cracked open from tree roots. And trees older than politics hugged our city, our neighborhoods, our main roads named for them: Cedar Lane, Black Oak Ridge, Maple Drive. Once my grandmother was driving me down the part of Broadway where traffic crawled over to one lane for the underpass. I was watching for the grocery store's flashing neon sign—red cutting shears snipping at a green dollar sign—when we slowed as traffic stalled. Ahead we saw men pulling another man from a wreck and propping him against the shaded breast of a sycamore, his body wilted, his face weeping blood. My grandmother's big hand covered my eyes as we passed. *Don't look* she said. When we drove out of the underpass, Broadway opened up again: K-Mart, the Family Drive-In, the vet's office, Shoneys. Business as usual. Grandmother told me to lay my head back and to be quiet. She wouldn't answer my questions about the man. The trees along Broadway blurred as we picked up speed, dissolving into sky. This morning I walk away from the yard signs and toward the ridge that rings my neighborhood. The little road that leads up to the apostolic church is steep, and I will labor to get to the top but when I do, I can catch my breath and watch my neighbors. I can see my own rooftop, my rusted chain link that needs replacing. I can think about how my grandmother failed to shield me, how the memory of that dead man marks me as surely as the trees on this ridge shade me now.

I chase the shady
side of trees where memory
lives in the shadows.

Mary Beth Whitley
Wrapped Cruciform

Karen Salyer McElmurray

The Roads She's Traveled

Those afternoons I climbed the steep hill behind Fannie Ellen's house, I believed in nothing much, but told myself the sound of the wind in those trees was holy. A dirt path led past a rundown hog pen, then disappeared as I pulled me and my notebook up, foothold by tree root. The world I'd known so far had not been kind. I'd had a childhood of sorts, one that nearly ate me alive. I'd given up my son to Social Services for adoption, and since then I'd filled up my loneliness with partying hard, with grief and confusion. At twenty, I was trying a different life on for size: living with my granny in Johnson County, in eastern Kentucky, while I attended community college. I climbed, surrendering to the sting of briars, counting myself wise with the few trees I could name. *Sycamore. Chestnut. Tree of Heaven.*

At the top of my climb was a rock-cliff where I sat looking out over the valley. Right across from Fannie Ellen's house lived distant cousins—Sue, married to a laid-off coal miner; Faye, who owned the country store. In my notebook I drew maps of the world as I knew it. *Jenny's Creek. Bull Creek. Puncheon. Water Gap. Abbott Mountain.* A two-lane, Highway 1428, cut its way through the valley, leading a few miles to the town of Paintsville in one direction and more miles to Prestonsburg in the other. Headed west on 1428 I'd once seen coal trucks dumping their loads during a strike. Riding the other direction on 1428 was a hole-in-the-road called East Point and a cut off to land Fannie Ellen owned—Bear Hollow, where she'd been raised.

Fannie Ellen said she wasn't brave enough for hill climbing, but we'd walked Bear Hollow more than once. It was land that had belonged to her grandparents, the Johnsons. There she showed me greens: *Poor Man's Bacon, Creasy, Dock.* Bear Hollow was her place of wishes when she was a girl. There she'd dreamed of being a nurse, an ambition she gave up when she chose to marry my grandfather. Good women, she said, rose up at daylight and prepared their houses in the ways of the Lord. I had no idea what good meant. My own beliefs were a mix of all the books I read—everything from girl mysteries to Russian novels to histories of the martyrdom of women saints, though my own version of God was simple enough. God was made of thunderstorms, art, and, as I looked out over the valley, the power of family history. I loved the stories I knew about the women I came from. There were strong women, granny women, even a tale about a bearded woman who ran off to join a traveling carnival. *Armentia George. Exer. Nethaladia. Ida Mae.* I wrote their names in my notebook and made up tiny stories about them, wishing I was them.

I supposed I'd be a good enough woman, sooner or later. Nights I slipped out and left Fannie Ellen sleeping, took rides around the lake in the next county. Other nights were brown bag and dancing at Marlow Tackett's Country Palace, up toward Pikeville. I took rides in a coal rig with a driver named Little Boots, who laughed as I took the gears through their paces. On my rock cliff, I told myself I was a seeker after an infinite quiet, but I knew the truth. I was always ready for a fight, as ready to head off into some big city as I was to stay put in Hagerhill. Some days I felt like I had some idea of the woman I was becoming, but most days I was a misfit, and I liked how that felt like I was a stone in a Mason jar, a too-big ring on a finger. As the sun slipped low over the valley, I sat awhile, looking out on a world I wanted badly to understand.

**

The first real short stories I wrote were based on who I witnessed in those little eastern Kentucky towns. I wrote a story about a girl named Mary Ruth who worked at Murphy's Dime store and loved the sound when she worked alone at night and wound up all the musical jewelry boxes. I wrote about a collector of dolls, about a lover of snakes and Jesus, about a guitar player at a church that allowed no music. As time passed, the women I wrote drifted through the world much as I had. In a magic realist novel set in the Great Depression called *Strange Birds in the Tree of Heaven,* Ruth Blue leaves her family behind to become a teacher of tap dance for a program sponsored by the Works Progress Administration. Leah, a lost girl in a short story called "Remember Who You Are," panhandles for spare change on a St. Louis street corner while she sits and feels her baby's heartbeat for the first time. And Miracelle Loving, in a more recent novel called *Wanting Radiance,* travels from east coast to west, from Fairbanks to Miami, telling false fortunes for a living, prophecies she desperately wishes were real. The women I wrote were uncertain of their lovers, their homes, sometimes their next meals, and I encouraged them as they rode miles towards futures they couldn't see, or hitched rides along strange highways. Their journeys seemed to have no beginning, no middle, no end, and I let them wander, seeking exactly who they might someday become.

**

When I left Hagerhill, I went to this college and that. I earned one degree, then another, and another. I began to throw my hat in the ring for jobs, conference presentations, and publications. But I always came back, awake or sleeping, to the land of my ancestors. I dreamed about crossing the creosoted bridge in front of Fannie Ellen's house. I dreamed of the stone foundations of my great grandparent's house up Bear Hollow. I craved eastern Kentucky like it was the one good meal that could satisfy me. I drove the long miles like they were hunger.

Soon Fannie Ellen's house was long gone and she was in nursing care, where she passed at ninety-two. My mother was in the final stages of Alzheimer's in another nursing home. Granny and Pa, my aunts, all were gone. When I visited Eastern Kentucky, I drove past my maternal grandparents' house, but it, too, had changed. Distant cousins lived there, and the Pentecostal Holiness Church across the road had become a car sales lot. In Hagerhill, house and hill were now under asphalt and it was hard to see where any of it used to be. I stayed as many days as I could on those trips, trying to hold that world on my tongue like communion. At the door to a house up Bear Hollow, a blonde-headed woman peered around a man in cowboy boots, her eyes narrow, sad-looking. At my mother's nursing home, a blind, one hundred year old woman looked out over the empty dining room tables. *Lord, honey,* she said. *Look what they done to them mountaintops.* I gathered memories like they were photographs from which I could sketch the world I'd left behind.

***

The women who inhabit my fiction and nonfiction—*Leah, Sarah, Ruby, Ruth, Pearl, Lory Llewellyn*—keep a toehold on belonging in the world. Theirs are stories of loss, hurt, and damage that can seem insurmountable. The stories are grief, rage, even madness. If there's a common denominator for these women, that one word—*journey*—covers it best. The women on my pages travel the literal miles of highways, the stumble of dirt paths, or the perimeters of rooms in houses they seldom leave. In my mind, they are inhabitants of far distances they must have to survive. They inhabit small spaces they struggle to escape, be they the heads of hollows or the confines of their own sorrowful hearts.

Some find the women I write helpless. Why, they want to know, don't they just *get on with it?* The *it* that needs getting on with amounts to surmounting depression, letting go of the past, or maybe just finding a good therapist and a few pharmaceuticals. Once I wrote a character who spends a long night in a bar grieving the lover who just slapped her across the face and kicked her out. When she leaves the bar she trips, falls. She doesn't bother getting up, but sits staring at a fistful of dirt. *What,* a workshop peer wanted to know, *is all this silly business about dirt anyway?* The women I write are moreso held fast by their lives than helpless. They are fierce fighters, whether the fight is inside themselves or out. They long for roads that take them nowhere as much as they long for ones that might take them to homes they've known. They are women who try mightily to find the selves they've lost or never had in the first place.

***

Two summers ago when I visited Kentucky, I rented a room at Jenny Wiley State Park. That morning I rode around town, had a meal at Billy Ray's, then took the old road beside what used to be my mother's house.

In the afternoon, I hiked in the park, climbed a hill to an unmarked grave—the wife of a soldier. What I saw from that spot was an Impressionist painting—a blur of ridge and lake and hills, and beyond that, nothing and no one else. Back to the lodge, I sipped wine at the karaoke bar, watched bad television in bed. But there's always more truth than not-truth in stories. That night I left the sliding door open onto a little balcony, even though it had begun to rain; a mist seeped over the lake and into my room. Under the covers to stay warm, I huddled up like a burrowing animal, as if I was hibernating.

In my burrow of sheets and blankets, I felt cold fingers reaching inside the blankets and sheets, caressing the back of my neck. The mist took on a ghost-shape, telling me to get up, close those sliding doors, and turn on the little electric stove by my bed. *Just sleep now,* she said. *Sleep and see what you can see.* Soon I was deep enough asleep to travel the highways and old roads I used to drive. One of those roads became an arm, its skin so translucent, I could see through to the veins. The hand belonged to Fannie Ellen. Like she'd done in the waking world of my past, she signaled that I come along with her. *Follow me,* she said, and so I rode along. This time what I rode on wasn't any road at all but a river, made of the blood of my kin. Their blood became my blood and soon I was dreaming of hills. Hills become mountains. Mountains, some of them ravaged, showing no sign of life. Some of the mountain were as round and full as a woman's belly, body-mountains from which so much wanting was yet to be born. Some of those mountains were me. My own body, an eco-system made of trails and rivers, trees, and plants. *Ginseng. Goldenseal. Yellow root.* The names tasted rich in my mouth.

***

Once a fellow writer wrote me after reading a draft of *Wanting Radiance.* He worried that readers would likely wonder why late-thirties Miracelle Loving, the main character, hasn't married and settled down yet. That question opened up others for me as I wrote and rewrote Miracelle's experiences. *Why choose riding the roads over a home? How do highways sound at night? Why choose strangers to fill up your heart rather than safety and love?* They're all questions I asked myself until I was forty-five and made the choice to share my life with a partner. They're all questions that have found a home in my continuing exploration of what makes a journey at all when it comes to writing stories, fiction or nonfiction. In my earliest workshops, we discussed *journey* in prose, and I learned important craft tools. *Narrative arc. Structure. Plot.* I learned that the dictates of plot aren't easy. *The king and the queen die,* is no plot at all, but *the queen dies and the king dies of grief*—that's a plot.

Are women's lives always that clear? Mine certainly hasn't been. If I ask Miracelle Loving whether her journey has been straightforward, she'd be sure to say no. She might well describe some dark night ride on a highway she took on a whim, a whim that led beyond the highway to a two-lane, then on from there to an unmarked gravel road and some juke joint with a broken marquee that flashed on and off, then stayed off as she decided to get just one drink before heading on her way. Who knows what could happen next? That's Miracelle's story, and it was my own, for years and years. Sometimes, I've come to think, an ending might well come before the surprising turn in the road, the middle point. The opening might end up being on the last page, just as the door to the run-down bar opens. *Beginning. Middle. End.* Do women's bodies follow clear paths, in their pursuit of pleasure, in their birth-giving, no less the arduous paths we take toward becoming ourselves?

***

I still wait for the eastern Kentucky earth to tell me something. I grieve for the land that no longer exists, and the land that is, mountains razed by highways, highways slashing through the memory of wilderness. I grieve memories and the people long gone. *Gone.* I am gone, too, in ways. I have chosen a different path than the one Fannie Ellen might have wanted for me. I rise up with good daylight, but it's to write sketches of what was, and stories about what might be. I'm a seeker. I drive home to Kentucky again and again, trying to summon ghosts, ghosts of mountains razed from the earth, all the places that once were. Like Miracelle Loving says, as she contemplates the places her journey toward peace has taken her, "I didn't know of what I was more afraid—roads out, or all the roads leading inside." I don't much know either, but I take the next turn, and the one after that.

Patsy Kisner

What I've Learned

Winter coughs.
After all, it is
December, and now
a dead deer
lies above the field,
the death by our
own hands
to feed ourselves.

Last August I
mourned the eerie
vultures that flared
from the ditch
every time
I walked
the road.

I couldn't bear
the tufts of hide,
shattered bone,
souring scraps
of flesh that,
given time,
the vultures
did their due
and erased.

I secretly mocked
the blood-red
marbled head
of the vulture.

How bitter now
to have felt superior
to something
that I'm not.

Patsy Kisner

October

A cold air
stirs.
Goldenrod bend
and weave.
Crickets scuttle
beneath
the screen door.
I light
the flame,
wait for the smell
of summer's dust
burning
from the heater.

Leatha Kendrick

All This Life Later

Fall stepped among the crickets' singing.
It's cool and slender toes waded flower stems
that October. My newborn daughter's head
rode against my shoulder,
heavy as a moon   luminous.
How could I believe I could decide on love
when its flood coursed through my resistance
like light   like death plowing toward me?

All this life later, death plows me still,
still I half-refuse the light,
my daughter a moon risen   turned away
toward her own daughter's running form.
In this small late yard a cricket saws its song
from the bank of asters nearing autumn bloom.
A second cricket answers, chirring in the zinnias,
a grating grace.   Love
is always a decision   and everything
depends on the tiring hand that cups a heavy head,
on the deliberate   softening of the clenched jaw.

Soon I will be a stone given back to ground,
dust taken up by air. Though bits of me swirl
deep in my daughter's
                    daughter leaping forward,

all I have is this –
storms and hatred, fire and melting poles,
this weight of love
to cradle, to choose   against the will
        that would set it all down.

Leatha Kendrick

The Door

Chaos is at the door
the more than I can do
the all I haven't done
the person who needs more.

At the door
in my friend's face
In the fear
that drove her out
that drove her here.

I can't, I say,
when she's standing there.
I can't, I say,
and unlock the door
to let her in.

I stand and cook the food
I had refused to make for us.
I listen to her talk.
I watch the dark
take up the yard outside.

I set the plates,
I lay the bowls of food.
Each thing in place
its color and its scent.
Eat, I say.

[and I say, *Eat*]

Leatha Kendrick

I packed my hinty-jinty, my wondrous

foolish livery box, and set out on a journey.
Part star-nosed mole, part fox, part
galaxy, I was, and something else
I hadn't got to yet,

(yes—white-haired as I was,
I hadn't found the rest
of me) and thus, the road, the goofy case
that held no suits except diamonds and clubs,
and a pure-suit of heartfelt acts

and spades to plant some bulbs
for blooming in another year
(and, yes, maybe a swim-
suit found its way
among the underwear and socks
and mouth-bent toothbrush

tucked in there). I set out
at a walk, the day was hot,
the finches sang, crows honked
and squawked like taxis in the air.
Just another day, and me
for once in no hurry.

CJ Farnsworth

Students will draw conclusions about WV from various types of charts, graphs, models, maps, pictures, artifacts, and timelines

When I found the boots
I knew so I put em
in a brown paper bag
I was huggin to my chest
as boy with face smudged up black
wore his momma's grandaddy's
hard boiled minin hat with one a them
carbide lamps...freckled, pushy
boy came wearin a coonskin
cap cause (he said) Daniel Boone
sat way up his family tree
...stringy red-haired girl dangled
a mustard seed pressed
in wax tied to a string
between her rickety finger
and thumb...boy with hair pokin
his eyes stopped at each desk
in case we were wantin to touch
his (Shawnee he swore) arrowhead
and some milky-skinned girl
brought her great granmomma's
milky white weddin bowl
...a'course fat jokes girl
stacked up some apple cake
for us to scarf and sad girl
with her too small shirts
clenched a jar a string beans
so hard I was thinkin the glass 'd break
when she was sayin her family's
been puttin up since God
was a boy...then struttin Tom
with shirt collars held up
a gold-framed black-n-white
of a bearded man
was in his daddy's line
with dark holes for eyes
said he kept up the govnr's office

for seven days straight
said didn't they look alike
and wiry Billy got some special
permission to bring thick brown
bottles a beer no one had drunk
…some rusty old railroad spikes
spitoon, musket gun, musty old quilt
…til when they finally called on me
I'd hugged my bag wet but I drug
it up, took out my own momma's
Go-Go dancin boots she said
she wore fore settlin down
I said they were such pure white
I thought they could fly
and she said you take those boots
and you show 'em and you tell 'em
soon as they fit is when
you're fixin to fly

CJ Farnsworth

Black

When I was age almost,
a Bobby came honkin'
in his daddy's blue Buick
Mama said you won't be
seein that boy again
he can't knock on my door.

At home no boys
came through cause
there wasn't much more
than beds, Mama's scarlet
Laz-y-boy, day old rolls
stuffed in the crumby
bread drawer.

Once a dark black boy
smart as a whip
funny as a strip
came sat on my stoop
when I was age not yet.

He stood taller, smiled
whiter than our front
storm door. I chipped
black paint off the rusty
stoop rail and laughed
sounds I never heard
before while mama rocked
that Laz-y-boy til the sun
plunged underground
an the neighbors lit up.

When that boy said 'night
right in my ear, I watched
him walk down the street
til I could see no more
then Mama sent me in
to the bath til just as I slid
a thin cotton gown

on my warm, damp skin
Mama came racin with a bag
a'them day old rolls
an never again did
that bright black boy
stand on my stoop.

More weeks into summer
I wondered why out loud
and Mama said yours
ain't none of that matter.

CJ Farnsworth

Uvalde

My son is cutting grass.

I can see his lips moving
along with whatever song
pumps into his head
as he tries to perfect
the light and dark
pattern in the grass.

He is about the same age
in-between I was when my mother
threw a glass candy dish
across the brown pall
of our living room, just missing
my left cheek.

As I watched her pick up
every shard of green coin glass
I could not imagine then
the fear and sadness
always in her grasp.

I cannot imagine now
the mown lawns
the blown glass
the shards of rage
too slick, hot, and sharp
to touch, the cutting
and cutting of dead patches
where nothing sweet
is like to seed, where so many
raw hearts stopped
stopped going great guns
stopped Texas cold.

Kari Gunter-Seymour
Rite of Passage

Renée Stewart

Texas (Song)

She was 10,
Balloons at the door
Artwork on the fridge
At the end of 4th grade
A whole life to dream for

Mom and Dad said
She couldn't wait for summer
Said her laugh was contagious
Her light shined so bright
All taken from her

CHORUS

Why won't this change us?
Why won't we let the pain in
Let it rearrange us?
We've been here before
The wolf's at the door
So we back down
All we do here is pray
But there's no more birthdays
In that Texas town

He was 10
With his hair slicked back
A wild-eyed grin
He liked to dance
He could run so fast

Mom and Dad said
He was the sweetest boy in his class
Every kiss, every hug, every moment of love
They want everything back

CHORUS

Why won't this change us?
Why won't we let the pain in
Let it rearrange us?
We've been here before
The wolf's at the door
So we back down
All we do here is pray
But there's no more birthdays
In that Texas town

REPEAT

All we do here is pray
But there's no more birthdays

Randi Ward

Conch

Brutal backyard
years of railroad
sleepers oozing
coal-tar creosote
across your cracked
mouth never silenced
your secret ocean.

Marie Manilla

Bimbo and Smitty and Bags

I spied on them from behind the magazine rack inside the pharmacy. The pharmacist's wife spied them too. She groaned and more vigorously wiped down the soda fountain counter. Across the street, the GVM, Gallaher Village Men, sat on the cement wall in front of the grade school my father had attended four decades earlier. They weren't men yet, the line of boys that included Bimbo and Smitty and Bags. They were high schoolers ranging from fifteen to eighteen, a ragtag crew of longhairs who wore patched bellbottoms and Army jackets, eyes often glassy from pot. They were routinely blamed for minor mayhem and petty thievery: shoplifting beer, knocking down street signs. Mostly they just loitered on that wall, or the one in front of the branch library, watching the city bus load and unload passengers at the pharmacy bus stop. I never saw them get on the bus. I don't think they rumbled with other local gangs: the EEBs, for example, East End Boys. This was the early seventies. Boys no longer sported ducktails or folded cigarette packs into their t-shirt sleeves. These were no Marlon Brando wannabees. I don't know what they wanted to be. I don't think they knew either. Maybe nobody did as Nixon sent boys to Vietnam: 334,600 in 1970; 156,800 in 1971. Why get on a bus when your future wasn't in your own hands?

Girls in my seventh-grade class wore copper POW/MIA bracelets engraved with the names of missing soldiers. Every night I watched war footage on the news with my father as anchormen tallied American dead. My two oldest brothers were eighteen and nineteen. They weren't aimless. One was in college. One joined the Army instead of waiting to be drafted, a little power grab. My parents drove him to the airport, Steve in uniform with a buzzcut. I often wonder what parting words our veteran dad imparted, if he offered any. He did not cast many pearls, at least not to me. If my parents fretted over Steve, they hid it well. Now, I understand, Mom was surely praying for him as she washed supper dishes, darned countless socks. Dad likely offered rosaries. Had sympathetic night terrors on his son's behalf.

But at the time their silence to me meant indifference. One Sunday I cut through the basement where Dad was watching football, Army versus Airforce. "Who you rooting for?"

"Airforce." Dad was a WWII airman.

I pictured Steve in his Army fatigues. "Figures."

"Marie!" It was a rare rebuke, and I deserved it, but I truly didn't know how my father felt about his son. How he felt about any of us, really.

The GVM crushed on older girls like my sister and her best friend Terry. Tried to flirt with them as they strolled through Gville. They didn't flirt with me, thankfully, which made it easier to sidle up to Bimbo that summer night he sat on the school wall, alone. Moths flittered in the streetlight beam encircling him. I'm not sure why I crossed the street, something in his posture perhaps, his downcast head. He spoke in code about his sister's death. "She kicked the bucket," he said, the first time I'd heard that euphemism. It took a minute to understand what he meant. Behind him, empty swings on the playground swayed. "She died?" "Yeah." He knocked over an imaginary bucket with his sneaker. Maybe he was bullshitting me, but I believed him. I believed the sadness in his eyes.

Or maybe he had no sister and what he mourned were his options. His birthdate that could be plucked from a blue capsule in a lottery. I had no such worries, at thirteen, when my favorite t-shirt was a yellow smiley face. I wore my sunny future like a brag.

Within a few years they were gone, that wall of boys. Some got into deeper trouble and were offered the choice of Army or jail. Smitty supposedly drowned shortly after graduating high school. Bags died of cancer in his twenties, misdiagnosed by the military. By the time his mother got him home it was too late. I recently found a death notice for Bimbo, though I'm not sure it was him. He died at fifty-three of some lingering illness. The obituary listed two live sisters. No dead ones.

Steve made it home alive. He learned to fire mortars. Played war games in Hawaiian terrain that was similar to Vietnam's. Sent blue airmail letters home that were left on the kitchen table for anyone to read. I don't remember specifics, but they were well-crafted and funny. Our family often used humored to deflect having to feel. Once, my parents had friends over for dinner. Maybe the Gadbuts. The Crickmers. Mom joked that Steve was living the high life in Oahu. "I'd like to have that job." Her voice dripped sarcasm. It angered me to hear her say that, to see her make that face, especially with Steve's airmail letter tucked between the saltshaker and napkin holder. As if he were boarding at the Royal Hawaiian, sipping a Mai Tai, not dreading the thought that he might be sent further west.

Or maybe Mom was deflecting too. Avoiding the possibility of her son being one order away from Vietnam. Conjuring a cushy tour during her prayers enabled her to fall asleep. Maybe her prayer made it to him and one night he left Schofield and thumbed into town. Ordered a drink in that pink hotel and strolled outside, found a wall to sit on, Diamondhead in the distance, and beyond it nothing but ocean. Maybe his mind drifted on a breeze, and Mom's prayers, carrying him mile after mile to the sun-drenched west coast, over desert and mountains, until he reached West Virginia, then Gallaher Village, where a row of boys sat on a concrete wall, dreading futures they could not possibly foresee.

56

Jane Hicks

Tobacco

I.
The tobacco of my childhood hung whispery and dry
in the rafters. No fires or flues like in low country,
only woodsmoke drifted up from the house stove
lingered outside the work shed. The November rains,
sharp and flinty cold, brought the dried leaves into case,
pliable enough to be handled on a human assembly line
denuding long stalks of lugs, long red, bright, and tips
graded and gathered into hands – bundles tied at the top –
packed on flat wooden baskets, piled higher than our heads,
we children the proper weight to compact the crop.
Hands gummy from sap, an ever-present nicotine high
helped warm our sneakered feet on the dirt floor.

II.
Wood smoke and dried leaves hung inside the shed
of an unfortunate first marriage. A wood stove and concrete
floor, an upgrade, my ability to tie a perfect hand of tobacco
my saving grace among people who scorned my bookish ways.
The flat baskets now head high and packed down with weights
built for such endeavor. Hands gummy, nicotine buzz,
tobacco dust all paid tuition and student loans.
Dried leaves and wood smoke,
the dry, the dead, and the burned.

III.
December howls outside, dried leaves and tobacco smoke
hang in the rafters of the growers' warehouse. Stand beside
crops as buyers follow auctioneer up and down long rows
of tall baskets, his chant echoes through the cavernous
tin-topped market. A bright smile might boost the price,
blonde head toss and low slung jeans sell
the nicotine buzz to buy an extra book, new tires.

IV.
Dirt floors and sheds gone, the concrete floors abandoned,
warehouses stand near-empty. I divorced the scent of
dried leaves, wood smoke, and nicotine. Left behind
the cold work of November rain and December wind,
an enterprise centered on smoke, the dead and dying.

Jane Hicks

What I Learned

The secret life begins early. —Billy Collins

I learned a lot in school. Oh, I know,
we all did, but I learned that some daddies
left for work and came home every day.
That some daddies hugged and kissed children,
helped with homework, and declared
their children beautiful and smart.

I learned that not all daddies had a white robe
and peaked hood in the trunk of their car, or
that many children were driven in their daddies'
car, not locked out.

I learned that some daddies laughed
with their children, played games.
My friends' daddies went to PTA
instead of cursing it as meddlesome,
and some daddies even sat and talked
without swearing or preaching about communists.

I learned some daddies drank too much, some daddies
never came back. Some daddies had belts and switches,
but never left welts and cuts to keep a child from school.
Some daddies woke crying from war dreams, but arose
to take children to church.

I learned, at school, by listening, that a daddy
most often was a good thing
and I learned to be sad.

Jane Hicks

Spotlight
—November 23, 2016

Under the one pink light of
an ultrasound room, my day
took an outlandish turn.

I clutch a gel-sodden towel over my breasts.
The lone light becomes spotlight, as if
scripted stage direction. The doctor,
young and earnest, enters,
hands me a dry towel, averts his eyes.

I re-cover. He takes my free hand,
delivers bad news: a tumor, small,
at eleven o'clock, very suspicious,
biopsy urgent. He walked over
from the hospital late on this
afternoon before Thanksgiving to spare
his nurse a grim task.

Scheduled and released, I huddle
in my car, take stock, cancel my shopping,
cancel thanksgiving, crank up music
and drive, and drive, and drive.

Frauke Palmer
Enchanted Forest

Lisa J. Parker

Big K Radio: Snow Day
—*for Laura*

My sister wakes me to heavy snow, her small belly
in my face as she leans over me to pull back curtains
on the window above the bed. We squint sleep away,
stare at the strange gray of pre-dawn,
listen to the pelt against glass.
We drag Grandma's quilts downstairs, watch
the window for first dawn when we can wake
our folks without trouble. We carry the radio with us,
creep the knob through the static and crackle of AM stations:
Roger Miller sings, *I'm the seventh out of seven sons*
my pappy's a pistol, I'm a son of a gun, a commercial
for Broadview Auto & Truck Service, finally land on
Big K Radio, Red Shipley's "Rise, Shine, Feel Fine"
and pull quilts tighter around us, waiting
to hear him say, *Fauquier County schools closed*,
an eternity of Porter Wagoner's "The First Mrs. Jones,"
Conway Twitty crooning "Hello Darlin,"
and we lay in for the long haul.

I carry kindling over to the woodstove,
crumple newspaper on top of the silky bed of ashes,
throw oak twigs on top of cedar shavings,
light the paper. We hunker by the open mouth,
Laura's freckled cheeks flash orange and shadow.
Chins on knees, we listen to the hiss of paper and shavings,
George Jones and Waylon Jennings pass the minutes with us,
I add parched hickory pieces to the slow flame, watch bright
sparks like blazing dandelion heads blown
from the belly of the stove. Red calls early risers
to join the old boys at Frost's Diner for breakfast specials,
between belts of Patsy and scratchy recordings of Jimmie Rodgers,
he reads off the day's local anniversaries and Nellie Depoy's recipe
for potato salad surprise, talks about playing guitar once
with June Carter, the reduced prices at Lehew Well Drilling,
markdowns on pork butt and Domenico steaks at Glascock Grocery.

It's closing in on an hour when he lists snow totals
from Culpeper to Rixeyville, and we doze against each other,

pieces of our mother's baby dresses stitched around us,
soft quilt edges, rhythmic crack of fire and radio static,
and all around us snow covers the county,
falls against hills we'll climb and careen down
later when we wake again to kettle whistle and Loretta Lynn,
familiar footfall overhead, skillets shuffled across burners,
smell of coffee and fried potatoes.
For now, we sleep at the mouth of the stove, music
of Nashville and Bristol beaming out of the farmhouse radio station
at the edge of town, above the Blue Ridge foothills, past signs
for polled Herefords and the Donut Xpress arcade and bakery.
We sleep while Red sips coffee, watches the slow stretch of dawn
through snow squalls, talks of *back in the day* as he drops
a Bill Monroe LP and plays "Footprints in the Snow,"
talks the county awake.

Lisa J. Parker

Hillbilly Transplant: In 72nd Street Subway Tunnel a Meditation on Home

Drive Old Leeds Road, curve and lift
of asphalt Daddy used to speed up for, drop
our stomachs like a moment's roller coaster,
at fork of Casanova Junction, a shock
of blackberry bramble, old Nehi freezer
where used to, there was a country store sold
the only black walnut ice cream in the county.

Drive past horse farms where pasture and orchard
turn open fields, the Airlie Estate where
the monied marry, where we crawled under
weak fence some nights in late spring
to night-stalk monster catfish from overstocked ponds.
Drive 605 to rutted cattle guard spots
where names meet rural routes, where horse farms
give way to small plots of corn, sustenance farms,
bricked silos and rusted tipples, down low roads
where the Thornton and Hazel Rivers meet at the foot
of Sperryville orchards, roadside stands of comb-in honey,
chow-chow and double wedding ring quilts
the tourists buy in fall. Drive the smooth, slow
wind of Skyline Drive where walls built by the CCC
still bracket the road, pull-off, and path.

Follow orange trumpet vine and wineberry bushes
till you hear the steady croon of the Shenandoah,
path of honeysuckle and black-purple pokeberry vine
to railroad ties laid into bank, creosote-soaked
staircase into cool grassy current,
let toes slide between rock shelf and riverbed,
crabcrawl where current is fast, find the place
where jutting rocks split water, the eddy and swirl
shallow enough for herons to stand watch.

Sit at the apex of water and rock,
breathe wet feather and river reed,
algae foam and mimosa blossoms.
Find stillness.

Open eyes.
Find yourself still city-gone.
Let yourself be moved
by wool coats, shouldered satchels,
unstoppable current of the mass.
Find a spot on slick metal pole.
Hold on.
Hear the whoosh as doors shut behind you.

Lisa J. Parker

Under the Sugar Moon

Path of gnarled knotting birch root
pushed up in pervasive, tangled tree webs,
scarcely a place for footfalls, but we walk it
at day's dimming, chase the gloaming,
when the heat haze has burned off
and we climb our way to pond perimeter
to perch a humped juneberry root, watch
for osprey to deadweight themselves from branches,
dive till they are just above surface and pitch up,
talons plunging the water to pull
unsuspecting bluegill from beneath.
We watch this till mosquitos have peppered us,
sound of flesh smacking flesh,
slapping the stealthy ones from each other's legs,
no one but us and what luminesces
from the hulking Sugar Moon, what calls
the sap and maple to life, to swell and spill
sticky sweet over early spring lovers
tangled in root and fern, phosphorescent foxfire,
all things breathless and incandescent.

Sue Weaver Dunlap

Enjambment

I meander along the branch bank early May,
search for lady slippers, find thick blankets
of mayapple, search my memory for the ditty
Mama sang to remind me about its poison.

I ponder Daddy in his shop, his years closing
faster now, sorting to his idle life. Miter box
and transom tools, three-foot level, and concrete
trowels go home with me. I build no shrine.

I linger at the spring pond, count trillium blooms
above the rocks, pale yellows, ground beauty.
Bloodroot juts out from the south slope, white
petals stark against a blanket of purple iris, wild.

I conjure Daddy bent over a wheelbarrow of mortar
mix, his concrete hoe at the ready for me to add water.
      "Back and forth, mix front to back,
      side to side, baby girl. Now, brick
      in one hand, trowel it on. Half a trowel.
      Some on the brick, the rest on your stack."

I capture my past up the trail, flaming orange azaleas
in the hardwoods, a fringed orchid safe in rich woods
dirt, ferns and ground moss its frame. I measure memory
scraping away rotting leaves from little brown jugs,

holding home.

Sue Weaver Dunlap

Breaking Bread

A young girl's recollection holds onto Grandma's kitchen,
the warmth of her cook stove lingers from breakfast
to supper, a tough pone of biscuit bread wrapped
in a bleached feed sack, saved for my brother and me,

this his last trip, a duty he no longer held, a breaking
of bread, placed on chipped plates, helpings of fried
salt pork back and potatoes, cooked slow in an iron pan,
onions sweet and tender. We sit warm at her table,

the flannel-backed oil cloth weary and worn,
our backdrop for the rare gift of food and love
from this quiet Grandma heart we never knew.

Sue Weaver Dunlap

This Morning at Dawn

Our front room holds quiet like an old woman wrapped shawl tight, deep-seated in her rocker, Poppy's Bible open in her lap. Faded eyes search out reminders of home kin sheltered behind a glass-doored curio. Tokens of past lives scent her heart. She conjures Charlie Goode's fingers pressing Prince Albert tobacco into his walnut pipe, his hands shaky deep into his own gloaming hour of leaving. Her well-worn small snuff tin holds its place high on its own shelf, this pocket tin long absent from her apron pocket, a thimble past quilting and mending chores. She waits for Mama to call her home with lonesome tunes on her harmonica, dark and old.

Omope Carter-Daboiku

Give Me That Old Time Religion

I don't remember my next-to brother Bruce as a baby; I just have pictures-in-albums memory of his infancy. I do remember that on June 2, 1956, I had slid from first pole position to a distant fourth in priority. I had been displaced as the first born by the first-born boy, as was the custom in my piece of Appalachia. We had just returned to Ohio from my father's enlistment in the US Air Force and our Florida residence. Pulling up to 808 South 8th Street in Ironton, Ohio, and seeing the new "home" with birds nesting in the soffits, I remember crying to "go home." I would be four years old that coming July; Bruce was born the day after our mother's own June 1st birthday. So, no need to say what that meant.

My brother and I grew close, even though we didn't play together. That was a quirk of the times; plus, the four years between us seemed like a gulf when we were young. I do remember that he was a busy, busy boy, running up and down the sidewalk racing himself in preparation for being a star athlete. Often, he was so exhausted, he fell asleep at the dinner table, his head falling into his plate of food.

As a youth, he was challenging responsibility always looking for ways to get out of work; I was constantly frustrated by his carefree "You're only in trouble if you get caught" attitude. Eventually though, after he became the oldest child in family residence, we found ourselves bonded by outsider perspectives of what being human meant, and our affinity for substances and music forbidden by our parents.

As an adult though, he was always hustling up a plan. We were taught to use our heads and our hands to sustain ourselves and generate cash for our needs and wants. So, even after developing AML—acute myeloid leukemia—he continued to maintain a local golf course and with his personal job benefits created outings for friends with discounted registration, and still made profit. Many years prior, he had an office cleaning business, teaching his sons the value of "a side hustle."

What he did not share about the AML diagnosis was the original prognosis of only six months. But with much prayer from family and friends and keen oversight by his wife of 40 years, he pulled out three years despite multiple crises and medical procedures. That was the miracle, like him leaping over the line of scrimmage to score that solo touchdown his senior year in the 1974 Ohio Class A football championship.

He lived his life to the fullest, managing to collect all the right toys— property on the Maryland shore, two boats, six grills (for his famous BBQ chicken and ribs sales), enough backyard to farm, multiple freezers to hold the bounty from the garden and the Chester River, along with a classic sapphire blue Rolls Royce. He lived as he told his mama he would. His generosity meant feeding his community on his birthday, making sure we enjoyed Maryland crab whenever we visited, and bringing loads of specialty foods when coming back home for Ironton's famous Memorial Day Parade. A hometown football and track star, one year he walked the parade route pulling his young son in a little red wagon, greeting buddies and hawking hot dogs topped with our mom's famous sauce.

So, it was all about to end as we accepted his illness and treatments that failed to restore his bone marrow and immune system. My son and I had planned to visit for Memorial Day and were headed to the shore when my sister-in-love called to say Bruce was having another crisis and asked that we postpone our visit. I went ahead and got an oil change for the car, intuitively knowing that we'd travel soon. The very next week, Sis called to say that it was time to come; within 24 hours, the family assembled by his bedside stunned at the rapid decline of his body. But, his sense of humor was still in form as he challenged his 93-year-old father to a foot race, and chided us for sitting around doing nothing; and, told us if we'd get him up from the bed, he'd find something for us to do! We told stories about our youth, remembering that our elders taught that faith is essential, and that laughter is good medicine.

The best gift my brother ever gave me was understanding my intense need to make sense of the world and human interaction. Being female meant being sidelined at home and in our church; the Apostle Paul's admonitions guaranteed that women would always know that their place was behind the men. I couldn't reconcile being expected to be perfect, and yet hide my flaming intuitive and creative talents. As the Vietnam War escalated, the Women's Movement emerged, and Black becoming beautiful, conflict between my parents and me sparked regularly in our household during my last years in high school. I began to search for deeper meaning for being as a person whose ancestors' skin and eye colors covered the palette of possibilities. After much research and reading, I came to define my spiritual worldview as non-European, based in meta-physics, which made sense since quantum theory says everything is composed of vibrating waves. For me, this completely aligned with Creator "speaking" the world into existence.

I began to use Yoruba cosmology (our father's ancestral lineage) to define my world, giving andromorphic identity to universal energies. Bruce was willing to listen and accommodate, not just tolerate. His support of me as his big sister struggling to find her agency in such turbulent times was knight-like, even though others might have thought we both wore tarnished armor.

As he faded, my thoughts reflected on the stories I tell in performance called "The Bruce Stories" that relay his affinity with fire and electricity, business acumen, and deep loyalty—the attributes of Orisa Shango. His exploration with fire and electricity nearly burnt the house down in one instance and blew him across the room in another when he stuck a car key into the wall socket; or, when he burnt his own tongue with Daddy's new car's cigarette lighter to prove that I was not the boss of him!

On Wednesday, while out eating crab in his honor, I watched the wind make white caps in the bay water as dark clouds gathered on the horizon; I told my designated driver to prepare to depart on Thursday, not Friday. As we were leaving the restaurant, far away flashes of lightening spread across the night sky. I got quiet and focused my breathing, anticipating the inevitable. At my nephew's apartment so generously vacated for our visit, I went inside quickly to lay down and let the thunderstorm lull me to restful sleep; but, instead was moved to speak aloud to the Universe, petitioning Shango, the owner of lightening, and Oya, the keeper of all last breaths, to escort my brother into the realm of the Ancestors, where I envisioned our mother waiting by the Pearly Gates with fishing poles in hand. I drifted off to sleep. In the middle of the night, a loud clap of thunder woke me, and I muttered to myself, "He's gone."

The call came at 8:33 Thursday morning. We had planned to depart at 10am, going past the house to say our goodbyes as we headed north. Instead, after dressing ourselves, we went to the Maryland Carters' house and gathered to dress and sit with our brother's empty shell, marveling at our collective strength and his fortitude. He had the strength and courage to wait until we were all together, even with my eldest child appearing virtually from Colorado.

Since Thursday, family and friends have sent condolences; but we don't need sympathy for we are not sad, nor sorrowful. We are elated by the quality of our family's adherence to tradition—gathering for the all-call, supporting each other's grieving process, eating food provided by neighbors, healing through the stories we repeat for the benefit of our next generation. So, they, too, will know that "old-time religion" is good enough.

Karen Whittington Nelson

My Sister is a Horse
—Elegy for Sara

Kindred spirits, our bond goes back eons.
Before we were born, I dipped my finger in ash,
traced her silhouette upon the wall of a smoky cave,
tattooed her likeness upon my soul with a blackened stick
and waited for her to find me.

She came like a miner escaping a collapsed life,
bursting through rock and time, leaving nothing behind
but rubble and reverberating silence.
My sister, a newly minted coin, stamped
from ancient elements,
torn from the belly of the world,
a wildling, quivering with freedom,
squealing her intentions, screaming my name,
bucking and farting, eyes rolling wild
like the ball bearings of a runaway train,
a too-hot boiler, snorting steam, ready to blow.

I whistled.

She slammed to a stop, pawed, turned twitching ears
my way and nickered in recognition.
We greeted, shared breath.
Her eyes softened; she allowed me
to love her.

Even now,
   on windy nights—
a nicker, soft as a bee's hum,
sweet, grassy breath tickling my neck.
I watch from the window as wispy clouds gather,
stretch their legs and race the moon across the sky.

Karen Whittington Nelson

Sunday's Pews

The preacher offered his calloused hand
and I gave myself over to him and God.
We waded to the center of the pool—
A dip, a splash, Hallelujah! Amen!
I was squeaky clean, beloved.
So simple a choice, everything made right…

Still, Sunday's pews were draped with
mummified old birds tough as stewing hens,
frowning and clucking their tongues
as we girls, on the cusp of spring,
rolled our hips and skipped down the aisle
to take communion.
Men with cigarette-breath coughed,
peered through the fingers of their cupped hands;
boys with nagging, innocent want
stole glances from behind hymnals as we passed.
Those who dared to touch the benches
polished by our swishing skirts reddened,
tucked tingling fingertips into their palms.

The congregation sensed a change of seasons upon us,
recognized our ripening impatience.
But we slid back into our pews
with every intention of giving the preacher his due.
But the morning was crisp and the sky, the sky—
oh, so blue…

We leaned toward the propped-open windows,
drawn to the essence of the morning, charmed by the
fragrant whispers and cheeky nods of the cherry trees
confined to the parish bower. In a gentle act of defiance
they spread wide their petal-plump limbs and offered a
glimpse of freedom beyond the church's dominion. Their
warm, floral breath tickled the sanctuary's stale, consecrated
air and melted the preacher's sharp barbs to butter—
sunny and benevolent as the holy light that streamed
through the austere panes, puddled on the pews and
dripped like molten bliss into the aisles.

Karen Whittington Nelson

Beloved Girl

I regret that my breast milk
was not sweeter,
that I never spun for you
a home of clouds,
spider silk and song.
That when you closed
the door on childhood
I let go your hand too soon,
failed to recognize
your seasons becoming
stationary,
your body struggling
to breach adolescence.

The missed distress calls,
those soft as bees' breath,
swept away
like windblown pollen.
The sirens, blaring warnings
too frightening to comprehend,
I shut the window against the din
and fed you tea and honey.

And you, listing in the current,
your body's tangled messages
snagged on rocks beyond
the reach of my net.
Your beautiful life
trickling to a slow swirl
in a stagnant eddy,
with blood
pooling around your ankles.

Alyson Annette Eshelman
Quiet Contemplation

Jane Ann Fuller

Jane

She's eighty-eight and doesn't care if she lives or dies, my mother
who says so while we visit Retha, who wants to know
why she hasn't seen the baby, so I hold his picture to her nose.
Get down, Izzy, says Retha's daughter, and the mini doodle nips her
knuckle as she swats the mutt away. *Would you like some sweet tea?*
Of course my mother doesn't care—her husband of sixty-eight years, already
dead—I know—I held his scrotum like I'd hold a sack of sapphires when
I helped him bathe, changed his *Depends*. I've always hated the smell
of lilacs, especially after rain. Once, I put her day pills in the night slots
and the Lasix made her *go* all night. Three times since May she's lost
her credit card, stuck to the bottom of a cookie box or gone between
cushions where her cats refuse to budge. I've tried to keep her company
with red geraniums, the paper's crossword on her lap by noon each day.
What else could she need? She still has her cyclone mind.
Her heart's jar of bees.

Jane Ann Fuller

The Last Year

every day of your life was a new life—
the crab tree's hard fruit, the doe's
cuspids, her greedy fawns. No
mystery without yearning. Why

I'd scoot you to the window where a moon's
hump back breeched, birds percussed on air.
Din of triangle, two-beat snare.
Maracas perched in trees whose

twigs scraped cabasa. Birds of your kingdom.
Grosbeaks. Chickadees. Never-
sated sparrows. Shrouded in mystery,
mystery vanished. *In the womb,*

you said, *we heard the beating heart.*
Today, I hear rain sticks. A crimson pair.

Connie Jordan Green

The Question of the Unknowable

Sitting beside you tonight as the horizon,
that sweet spot where earth and sky embrace,
vanishes from sight and stars pop out one
by one—unknown sparks falling into place
to form the familiar constellations, Mars
lingering in the arms of the poplar—I think
back on what brought us here, the years

of struggle, too little money and too many bills,
how morning came with its many tasks, evening
with its blessings, how we had no time to ponder
the unknowable, consumed as we were by children,
jobs, the farm with its urgent, unquenchable demands—
how time rolled us to this moment, time, that

disrespecter of wants and emotions, days vanished
like dry leaves in November wind, like chalk marks
in April rain, like a child's innocence, the two of us
nearing the end of the knowable, filled yet
by the wonder of all that is mysterious.

Connie Jordan Green

Rocks

[O]ur rocks / flourished with
no attention at all.
  —Jesse Graves

Our first and most lasting harvest was rocks—
rocks we picked up across the pasture fields,
heaved onto an open wagon hitched to the small
Farmall that chugged up the hills we had bought
as farm, rocks we unloaded to fill gullies
that rivered our ground, remnants of poor farming
practices and still poorer soil, a purchase we
in ignorance eagerly made, the yearning for
our own land a light that brightened those days
of clay-locked earth flailed with hoe, bean and tomato
plants doomed to struggle while we stubbornly
hauled rock after rock to a place in the shade
where only the lizards or occasional snake
saw their beauty and rejoiced in the abundant crop.

Connie Jordan Green

Finding Gratitude
—after Naomi Shihab Nye

Before you find gratitude, you must
know the grief of loss, must shiver
with winter winds. You must climb
the rocky precipice, hand over bleeding
hand, hope distant as the hawk overhead.

Before you feel sunshine, you must
shoulder through the dark fir forest,
the sweet smell of soft needles
unfathomable to your senses. You must
be the starving child with flies on his eyes
and know with certainty this is you,
too, know one breath fills all the world.

Before you find the sea of gratitude,
you must cross the desert of too much
bordered by the hutments of too little,
you must enter the heart of the prodigal
through the sweat of the faithful brother.

You must lie down with pain, clothe
yourself in its rough fabric and think
this is the feel of the future, you must
gaze over the plains to where the first
glimmer of daylight opens the door
through which gratitude glides, you
and gratitude recognizing one another
the way a mother picks out her child
from the crowd of faces packing the street.

Jonie McIntire

A Pragmatist's Love Poem

The oak tree in front of my parents' house has died.
The one we got married under. The one over a hundred
years old, branching right in front of the picture window.
Remember when you planted that maple after your father died.
How the tree barely lasted a season. Followed by
another sapling and then another. Until finally,
something took and we stopped associating it
with what we'd lost. Love is a natural law.
A sure thing predictable as gravity, sure
as two bodies in constant attraction, cores solid.
The farmer across the road knows a guy
who sells firewood. Asked my dad if they could
cut the tree down for free. A godsend. Left alone,
its hollow could crush the house entirely.

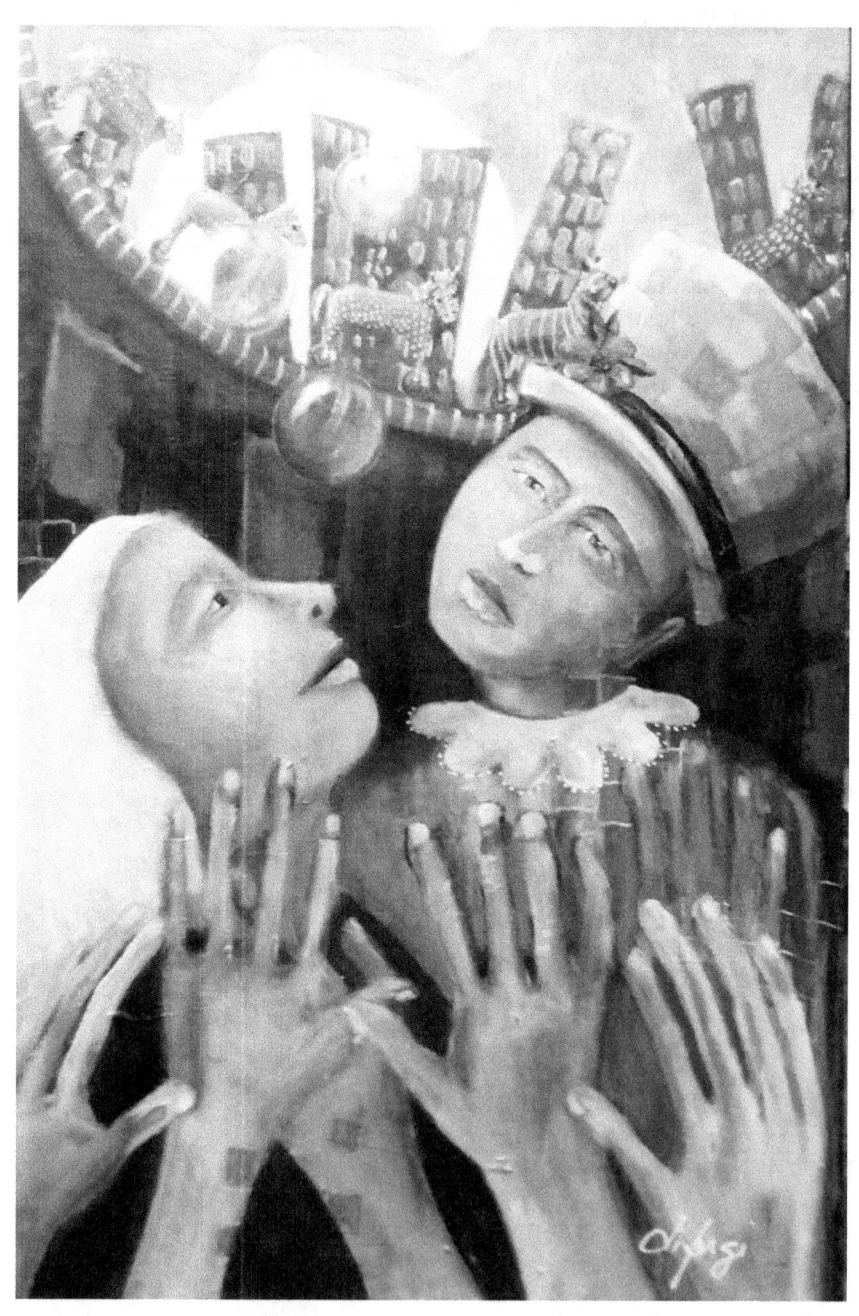

Diana Ferguson
Dare to Dream

Mitzi Dorton

The Robbery

Carolina examined herself in the wavy reflection of the mirror atop her oak dresser. She frowned as she unpinned her hair, and it fell in dark brown waves past her elbows. A few days ago, she had stuffed the down payment on their property in a little hobnail high heel shoe. That money was her ticket to buy the Model T, to take her family out of the confines of Moccasin Hollow and to buy a farm up north. Carolina had been distracted. The nosy ice man's wife had studied the rims of Carolina's little hobnail pieces in cranberry and turquoise, sliding her fingers, checking for chips, holding them up to the light and exclaiming how nice they were. Then, Carolina had turned around to retrieve the money from her brassiere to pay what she owed. That must have been when Old Lady Simms snatched it! The old woman talked out of both sides of her mouth, praising the pieces one minute and then scolding for not spending the money on food for the children. Just because she eyed our little ones in her mulberry tree. Why, any young'un might be tempted, the boughs speckled with sweet purple strands!

Carolina had admitted to neighbors she had forgone the store-bought bread to buy the what-nots, and perhaps Old Lady Simms had heard about it. Carolina's skillet-made cornbread was to brag about though. Her daddy had said as much today when he stopped by for dinner, and there was always plenty.

Then, her husband, Emory, had asked of its whereabouts. That was when she remembered stumbling, dashing up the steps. The shoe was there, among all the treasured pieces. At first, Carolina exclaimed, "Thank you, Lord Jesus!" Carolina picked it up and held it to the light…but it was empty. She remembered picking up each glass piece, the cranberry scalloped basket, the fan-shaped milk glass vase one by one. "Emory!" she hollered "It's gone!" Carolina's hands shook, as she turned each glass piece upside down, checking them again and again.

She clanked down a white enamel bowl on the oak dresser in front of her. Easier than drawing water from the well and heating it on the cookstove, she began the arduous task, brushing corn meal through small strands of her hair for a dry wash. She fumed. It was one thing to spend money on a necessity, and another to have a trickster like Old Lady Simms make off with your fortune! Carolina bent her head forward and grabbed the back of her hair over the bowl. Here I am looking for a better life for us. She pulled up a strand at a time and brushed it out, letting the meal fall into the metal bowl. Then, wrinkling her brow, she slapped the brush down on the dresser. To the devil with losses! Carolina stood up, went over to t the sewing basket and removed the shears. It seemed an evil thing to do in one way, as she stood before her reflection with an oil lamp burning on the table behind her, her chin stuck out, determined. Carolina dared herself.

She whacked the first section below her ear, as a gasp from her own throat mocked the sound of the brave scissors. The second chop, and a long piece of hair fell from her back beside the other one, landing on the floor. One side was long. She compared the before and after. There was no going back now. The third was easier. Immediately after the act was done, or crime committed as she thought of what her daddy would say, she felt a sense of both freedom and dread, as she tried to measure with a careful eye, to trim it up. She was the rebel of the family, and she nodded in approval at that thought. She would still leave the area when the full amount on the farm was paid at the end of the month, not if the Model T got sold though. She comforted herself, and pressed her cheek on each side, and she twisted her head to inspect for damage. Not bad! She thought she looked like one of the ladies from the 'Sears and Roebuck' catalogue! Someday she would put in an order for that model's dress, so soft and free flowing, the hem above the ankle.

Carolina left the house and headed toward the white cottage where she grew up. It was not far around the bend and up a steep hill. After she showed her older sisters her new bob and shocked them, (like she did when she eloped with Emory), she would pay Old Lady Simms a visit. Let her know she wanted the money back!

Carolina could hear the organ playing in the distance. Usually, that would be Mama astounding the chickens, who sometimes were the only audience. The organ was the only elegant thing they had, delivered on a flatbed wagon pulled by horses, an inheritance from northern Virginia from her mother's father. The echo bounced off the surrounding hills and down into the valleys of the hollow. One of her sisters must be fooling around, because she knew Mama was over at the church house quilting.

She could see Daddy ploughing near the last few rows. That meant he would be home soon. She wanted to pop in and out before he finished. Carolina knew he loved her, but he often seemed puzzled with her choices. He was proud of her mama, his bride, who had fine manners and searched in the Bible when guidance was needed. She was glad she had covered her head with a scarf. She waved at him, while swinging a feed sack in her other hand. She wanted to let her sisters know she was not a paper doll cut out of one of them. She sped up and took the wooden steps, two at a time, across the wide planked porch, and into the front door.

"Loou-cy!" Carolina called out to her older sister as she entered the kitchen opening the bag. "Don't look now. I bobbed my hair! It filled a whole feed sack!" She reached for a handful, pulling it out.

Instead, her mama parted the door curtain, "Oh Carolina, is everything okay?" Mama continued in almost a whisper when she noticed the haircut. "Are you alright, girl? I heard about the money being lost from Emory's pa." She spoke carefully, and Carolina could tell by the hollow stare she suspected her daughter might have some kind of mental imbalance, a nervous breakdown maybe.

"Yeah, Old Lady Simms pilfered around and snatched it up. I should've never let her in the door." Carolina, said, glad to switch gears and talk about the neighbor. Mama was not finished. She reached to feel for Carolina's missing locks as though in a trance. "Oh, Carolina," she barely whispered, "the Bible is again' cutting hair." Carolina turned and brushed away, "I thought you were quilting with the ladies."

"Three took sick this week," she murmured, still staring at this oddity, her daughter.

"I like the new styles!" Carolina replied, trying to recover and make a quick beeline for the front door in her flapper style hairdo, the smart pin curls toward her cheeks. Carolina stopped though when she heard the front door slap shut. She let out a gasp, the way she did when she snipped the first lock of hair. She prayed it was one of her sisters.

She had meant to be gone before Daddy finished his work. She heard the footsteps on the hardwood floor, shuffling across the living room and halting at the kitchen door.

He took one look at her, took a step backwards, sucked in his breath and wiped his eyes, as though he did not believe what he saw. Carolina's two long-haired sisters, Prim and Proper, as she never called them face-to-face, arrived at the other side doorway in time to view the consequences, as her mama pursed her lips and shot her eyes helplessly at them. Her father then announced in a heavy tone to Carolina that, "A woman's hair is her crowning glory, a sign of godliness." Then letting out his breath, he pounded on the door facing. He shook his head and leaned it on his arm in defeat. He turned and walked out on to the porch, and she heard the screech of the chains as he took a seat on the swing, then heavy sobs.

She knew it grieved him that she strayed from what he was used to. Daddy never did quite know what to do with her, she thought, but she had never heard him cry.

The sisters stood gawking at the side door, but when she started to leave, they jumped at Carolina. One in a tight coiled bun hollered out, "What fool thing have you done now to rile daddy?" The other, whose brown cottage loaf centered in the middle of her head, wobbled as she leaned forward to accuse Carolina, "You had to go and break Daddy's heart, didn't you? He's all torn up anyway about you taking off and leaving. Now, you've spoiled your honor and our'n too."

Carolina had delighted in dismaying her older sisters with their suitors, seeing their alarmed expressions as they watched her turning somersaults down the hill to show off her pantaloons. She knew neither of them had considered snipping their long brown waves, because she only saw them let their hair down in private, in their darkened rooms at night. She went out on the porch with her daddy and spoke her piece, "I need to find my own way with Emory. I am married; he is my man now. We will be back to visit. Our kin are here."

"We raised you to be a fine lady. Then you go and do everything you can to ruin yourself, and that boy you ended up with is no good. Mark my word, girl, he'll bring you to sorrow." He hung his head down and looked at his workworn hands, as though he considered on something hard to say.

Emory was her man. They had been neighbors growing up. Emory had been a rebel from the time he was small. He jumped out of the window of the one-room schoolhouse named for his ancestors and never returned. She sat right there in the schoolhouse when it happened, silently cheering him on, the schoolmaster grabbing a stick and chasing him out into the schoolyard. Emory never could read or write, and he sometimes even wrote his "m" as a "w" in his name, but he was not dumb. Nobody was better looking, and she had his two beautiful offspring. He supported her when she rode in the local fairs and horse shows. She never pretended to be delicate, and competition was fierce for her. She remembered Emory walking up to stand beside of her, looking up with a shy grin in support, and cocking up an eyebrow when they handed her a blue ribbon. Her man understood her! Daddy did not. Besides, Emory was her only match, in these parts.

Carolina then realized Mama had been standing in the shadow of the screen door. "Let her go. We've come as far as we can with her," she said to him. She stepped out on the porch and continued, "We'll miss you, Carolina. You will always be our baby girl wherever the moon is," she pointed to the white globe rising in the daytime above the mountain in the distance. "We'll always be connected under the same moon!" Carolina did not know where Mama summoned the bravery and why Daddy did not challenge it, but she was relieved by Mama's release.

"We'll be back. Our kin are here," Carolina assured them. Then changing the subject again after brushing Daddy's shoulder with her fingertips, as she started toward the steps, "Well, I'm on my way to tell Old Lady Simms that we know she stole our money."

"Wait, girl," her daddy looked up, with tired, pale blue eyes. "I was the one who took the money. I wanted to save it for you to buy Henley's property. I was going to make a down payment on it for you tomorrow, but the more I thought about it, knowing you and Emory, I knew you'd take off anyway on the rest of what you got, and let Henley's house go to the brush. It's a fool decision you are making, and mark my word, it will come back to haunt you. I only did this because I cared for you. Remember that, and don't forget where you came from." He dug in his pocket and reached out the money toward her.

Stunned, Carolina clasped the down payment in her hand. She murmured, "I won't forget," but on the inside she had a mixture of emotions, anger that her daddy thought he could control her life forever, sorrow for wanting to escape and leave behind parents who loved her in spite of her different mindset, and elation that the blessed money was in her hands again.

Carolina lit out down the wooden stairs and stuffed the money in her brassiere after she was out of sight. She pursed her lips while gazing ahead on the path before her. She was free. The moon, hazy in the distance, seemed almost as if a thin silk scarf veiled it for all the promise that could unfold.

Chrissie Anderson Peters

Then Your Tulips Will Grow

If deep frost doesn't come late, then your tulips will grow.
If your husband doesn't mow there, then your tulips will grow.
If the sun shines full there, then your tulips will grow.
If the mice and moles miss them, then your tulips will grow.
If you don't overwater, then your tulips will grow.
If your cats don't piss there, then your tulips will grow.
If the ghost of your Mamaw inhabits the space, then your tulips will grow.
If you curse your black thumb, then your tulips will grow.
If Mother Nature is in it, then your tulips will grow.

Roberta Schultz (Song)

Babushkas

Once upon a time,
back in the land of rhyme,
three sisters play out in the cold.
Their mama calls them in,
ties underneath each chin
large scarves in colors bold.

Babushkas in the yard.
Life never was so hard
as hand-me-down might seem.
They dance their over-sized dream.
Dance lightly, sweet Babushkas.

Coats hang below their knees,
scarves billow in the breeze
they stomp their circles in the grass,
stoop down to gather
every scarlet leaf and feather.
Mama's laughing through the glass.

Babushkas in the fall—
like tiny grandmas at a ball.
It must have been her treat
to watch her babies on their feet
just making up new dances.

Babushkas dance on still.
Kick up your feet there on that hill
where sun glints golden on gray hair.
Loose scarves are waving in the air
to welcome new Babushkas.

Roberta Schultz

Like the Sycamore Stands (Song)

Miss Sookie says, "this is the way to free time:
answer when asked. Never talk more than they.
Lower your eyes. Don't let your face ask questions.
Lean toward the light. There, you'll find words to say."

CHORUS

Like the sycamore stands
tall above all this land,
you can stretch out your roots,
little fingers and shoots
grow beyond all command.
By the water you'll rise. Periwinkle disguise.
Near the window you sing, little birds without wings,
of your home in the sky.

Miss Sookie says, "here is a drum, my children.
Shake up those gourds and play me a morning song.
Rattle your seeds, blast on those flutes, dear babies.
March to your heartbeat. You will be free ere long."

CHORUS

TAG
Freedom is a long hard ride.
Freedom is a gospel train.
Freedom is a banjo tune.
You know that freedom,
it sounds a lot like the blues.

Randi Ward
Miss Clara's Cairn

Rita Sims Quillen

Some Notes You Hold

—There were Native American tribes who built
platforms in their cornfields where the women
kept watch near harvest time, singing
continuously to frighten away animals.

On a barnwood stage built by their men
above a green ballet of corn and blue curtain of sky,
the women take turns, daylight to daylight
singing and clapping, beating drums
that take their men to war.
Deer and turkey stalk the rows
unless this symphony in the silks
lifts through the tree canopy like thin smoke.
Theirs is a holy chorus:
Wolf howl, cooing doves, hallelujah magpies
cawing crows answered in a minor key
chanting ancient sorrows to God and wind.

A small girl walks with her mother
for the very first time to the field
to learn what singing is.
This here is a note, her mother says,
and sounds out a perfect sweet C
with vibrato swift as hummingbird wings.
All you need to know of singing, she says,
Whether in church or corn:
Some notes you hold, some you let go.

I have never sung to corn
but have put everything else aside
to let my voice clear the air
slicing clean as the bone-handled knife
that freed the cob from the stalk.
Melody has broken bread and beans
delivered blood red baby tomatoes
to wide-mouthed chalices,
washed mud from squash and onions
soothed tender lettuce in its cool bath
pieced a day back together to a 4-beat line,
hummed the doxology of earthly delights—
all the savory songs of soil and seed.
Some notes you hold, some you let go.

Rita Sims Quillen

Prayer for Birds and Sunrise

Thank you for the porch facing east
where I watch each morning
God's hot palm rise
above the mountain's soft sides
fingers spread wide
against a grey pink canvas,
tender light building a silkscreen
to catch soft drops of worry, sorrow or regret
blown across my hot cup's surface.

May I hear forever the birds above
ones, twos, and triplets of feathered music
floating and darting the currents,
their notes an art song of holy noise
from ancient studios of creation
before love was a word, or grief,
before time became a ghost
breaking glass in the rooms upstairs.

Let the fingered dawn launch the raptor
to carry my heart to deepest secrets of trees,
my feet to the wild creek, my hands together
and head up, walking straight and strong
to fox den, bee tree, deer bed—
places where I wait for the truest rejoicing.

Rita Sims Quillen

Writer's Block

I am not writing today—
yet an exquisite red fox
dug for mice in the sawdust.
Pear blossoms opened fat silk arms,
caught the moon's overflow
pouring itself out
silver tea into the ridge's cup.

I am not writing now—
while the world masquerades,
sings a Spring serenade.
Wind whistles through
leaf litter ankle deep.
Trees wake and tremble with birded limbs,
leaf buds lifting like prayers.

I am not writing these days—
yet above me starlings ricochet
black boomerangs in cloud banks,
a squirrel prays for hours
atop a cedar fence post—
Vicar of the vines—
and absolves me for it all.

I am not writing today.

Lacy Snapp

Lullaby to the Decomposing Succulent

I didn't mean to kill you
so quickly.
But since I did, let me send you off
in style, in song,
a haphazard string of notes to guide
you to your eternal sleep.

I swore you would propagate.
So I plucked from your torso some healthy
limbs and barely tucked them
into a tray of loose dirt
in a sunny windowsill. Soil hugged
your sides like covers in the night.
Oh, you just wait,
I promised, *sleep for now,*
calm your breathing.

And you did. And you grew
little baby hairs of roots from your feet
and the day I noticed, I pressed
my face close to yours, hoping my hot breath
would wake you from
your sleep.
We are not here
for long. You or me.

So we made plans,
I planted you in a wide, shallow dish,
put you out on the front porch
to greet morning glories with your first breath
after each sleep.
Your skin turned pink,
pleased with the direct sunlight.

But with the first
frost of winter, oh, I tried to keep you safe.
Brought you in from the cold. But the warmth
turned you to mush in a few hours,
your kind rosette

face lost its shape in my hands.
Sleep now, we are not here
for long. I'm sure, I, too,
will follow your cue—warmth, to cold, to warmth.
From sleep, to this waking dream of climbing
roots and morning glories, to frost, then
warmth, then sleep.

Lacy Snapp

I Surrender My Garden to Her

That artistic, giant yellow and black garden spider
is a dangerous woman.
When male spiders court her
plucking the edges of her web,
they always have a contingency plan
an escape route
in case she is not flattered
by their careful
advances,
and instead seeks
to kill him

and eat him.

Care must be taken by people, too.
One should speak no name
around her web,
because if she spells it out
with her zigzag weavings,
they say,
that person
will die soon.

Superstitious of disturbing her web,
I have surrendered the far right corner of my garden
to her.
At night, after watering,
I press myself flat
against the house
to pass
as she restrings to snare her

evening supper.
I keep my distance,
some cherry tomatoes drop from vine
to the soil
in the corner I cannot reach,
now hers alone.

I think I understand—
though she will die with the first frost
of fall,
after a full summer of webbing
at dusk,
consuming those centers
only to rebuild
each morning
with fresh silk,
she holds on for as long
as she can.
She has an egg sack to protect.
Silken souls
in the thousands
tiny as dust
wrapped up tight
until their spring exodus,
soon to be
writers of creation themselves.

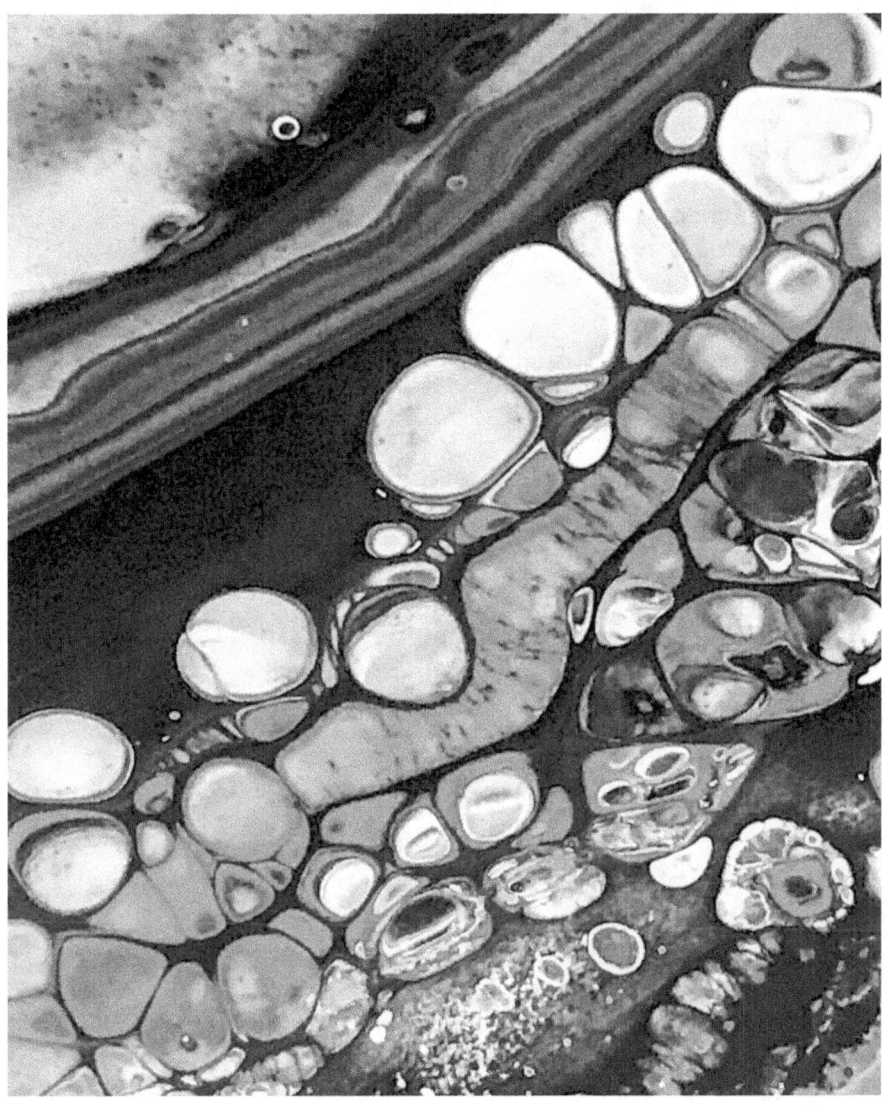

Jessica Held
Pebbles

Sylvia Bailey Shurbutt

Butterfly Days

Gossamer wings
     As up you float,
     Gold against a cerulean sky;
Translucent skin
     In shimmering sunshine,
     Here and there you flit alone,
Capricious flirt
     Among the blossoms,
     Sucking sweet nectar from pistillate petals.

Then down among the dung
     You sit to ruminate.

Sylvia Bailey Shurbutt

Vermeer: Three Paintings

Cool, quiet reality.
Woman in blue
      Delphic hue,
      Caught in a moment—
Forever to turn from your pewter flask
      To the window light.

Light and air,
Moisture one can feel
      Through paint and canvas—
      So Delft, the city,
Breathes in silence
While sun reflects from every brick and tile.

And maiden fair,
Ever to pour your jug of milk,
      Its liquid streams into an earthen bowl
You have no other thought
Save pondering
The liquefaction of the moment.

So each work
This brush has wrought
      Becomes far more than color and cloth—
      A link with Time and Infinity
A Moment forever

Sylvia Bailey Shurbutt

Country Fields, Intimations of G. M. Hopkins

Dapple down brown
    The sillion
Breaks each earthen clod
    Plow blade vermillion

Making rows
    Of parallel lines
        In neat procession,
    Geometric lines toward infinite space
        Progression.

Gaze in verdure wonder
    Scintillate sight
Till vision's blight by bright
And blurring sun
Brings Earth and Sky to one.

Katlin Brock

Home

Whether mountain or sea,
    You are adrift

You float on the surface
    Skimming the tides
    Which try to pull you back

    And forth
    In your mind, the subtle lull
    Of the pickaxe and the spade

The smell of salt
    You remember from childhood
    In the great smokehouses

    Where your granny
    Hid her tobacco pouch
    For her corncob pipe

Angie Dribben

I Like Neck Meat (1974)

This girl. My youngest. My wildest. My saddest girl. The only one still at home. Lenny was going to faint right here in the kitchen. Not talking about Barksdale, her boyfriend, but his momma.

"Her bracelets just chimed, and she said they are watermelon tourmaline," Lenny babbled on. "And her nails are all so rounded and her hands. Oh Momma, her hands the way they felt when she held mine. So sweet Momma. She's so giving to everybody."

I couldn't help it. I know I should've felt different about it. Instead, I was thinking of doing awful things to that tomato with the knife in my hand. Hangnails, fat knuckles, and all. As I laid the slice still smelling like vine on a butter biscuit left over from yesterday, I didn't even turn around and smile with Lenny.

"Momma, when you gone go on a date? Aunt Hazel's got one in mind for you."

Best just to laugh this off. Best not to give too many reasons. Best. Not to say I been on dates. I loved somebody. I had somebody keeping my heart warm even after all these years. And I was going back to them.

It sure ain't that Daddy of hers. Planted all those wild dreams in my head. And in hers. With his bags of candy for our girls every time he walked through the door. Young girls are so easy. Wave a Red Hot in front of them and they won't never think to ask why he can't stand up straight. Young girls take every sweet thing given to them like it's a favor when it's more like a worm on a hook. No, more like being gill-hooked by a worm.

"Momma, don't you want to be in love again?"

Sometimes I think it'd be easier to set her straight about love. How quickly who you think you love can change. Or what you think love feels like. Sometimes it's a way out like her Daddy was. Like Barksdale is. Sometimes it's a way in.

"Again?" It slipped out for I could catch it. I smoothed the small cornflower blue daisies down my dress. Tugged back on the fabric the same way it tugged at my hips. Way she was carrying around and that sweet smell spilling out her mouth, I think Barksdale brought her a home with a little buzz. I wondered if she was drunk enough to lose her hearing. Hoped she was. I don't know if it'll ever be right for her to know I wasn't in love with her Daddy by the end and best I could tell, he most likely didn't love me. You do right by people you love even when it isn't what comes natural. Didn't neither one of us do that. We needed each other to make a home and rent.

She didn't seem to have heard me, so I slid my glasses tight to the bridge between my eyes and squared up with her.

"Men ain't good but for one thing and I am too old now for that."

I knew Lenny didn't want to talk sex with me because she didn't want to talk about her having sex. I knew she was having sex though. In fact, I was worried soon enough the whole world would know she'd been having sex. The waist band of those hip huggers seemed to be yielding a bit to her belly. Folding over where it used to go straight up. She does have a fondness for the meringue off my chocolate pie, but still. I got an uncomfortable heat crawling up and down my spine these days. It's the way I know when something bad's coming.

I'd wanted all four of my daughters to finish high school. It's hard to get anywhere in this world without the right pieces of paper. Hard to get going out into the world. Hard to get anything. I want them to have their lights on all the time. All their lights, all the time. So far, not one has graduated. And probably not this one, my last one, either. The school wasn't gone let some unmarried pregnant girl sit up in English class. Who knew if Barksdale was going to take her on or not.

"Momma, you can't be too old for sex. Barksdale's parents are still in love. They touch each other's knees under the tablecloth where they think nobody else can see."

Lord, she done brought it up in my kitchen. In her Momma's kitchen.

"Girl, what you think you know about sex?"

Her eyes got so big I think her mouth fell off her face. She pressed herself so tight in the corner cabinets I thought she might disappear in them.

"Better still, tell me this, what do love and sex have to do with each other? No, tell me what knees got to do with sex?"

I stared her down as hard as I knew how. This conversation would be best ended. I wanted her to go to bed. But, this damned girl started twirling around again like I ain't said nothing.

"Oh Momma, she was so sweet. We all sat at the table together. She made this whole big meal for us all. Mashed potatoes and fried chicken and everybody got whatever piece they wanted and green beans and yeast rolls and buttered corn. Oh, and sweet tea!"

"Must be nice to have all that to fix your family." I was having a biscuit and a tomato out the garden tonight. I had to make the most of it when Lenny ate somewhere else. These were the nights I ate next to nothing, and Lenny didn't notice. Even when we ate together, it was always mostly her eating. She won't taking note of what was on my plate, only on Barksdale's Momma's.

"Oh Momma, she's so giving."

She reminded me of her Daddy and the way he'd get so carried away going on and on about how good something was or how bad. It was either, "Oh this job is going to change all our lives;" "You won't never have to work again;" or his most common, "I ain't gone work another day for so little as $2 an hour."

He won't gone work because he won't gone work and our lives won't gone change because my work alone wasn't enough to change them. Here she was just like him, all caught up on what she wanted to see, marry Barksdale and she'd have soft hands and pretty bracelets like his Momma. Not be all gnarled up and grayed out like me.

And also just like her Daddy, she could decide to hear what she wanted to hear and keep on getting it like she ain't heard a thing she didn't want to.

I tried to keep my eyes on my ankles busting out the tops of my old granny shoes, swoll from standing at the knitting mill all day. I both wanted to throttle her and didn't want her to ever know any different than this—spinning around the trailer's kitchen bigger than you'd have thought a trailer would allow. Love isn't enough to keep hands soft or tables full. At least not for people like us.

Being the oldest, I was the one to quit school in the seventh grade and help out when Daddy broke his back. Mama said it was branches broke him up on the way down. Seems more likely it was roots. Since he was cleaning a well when he fell to the bottom.

Daddy spent five years just laying on his breaks. He got real acquainted with time. Poking around behind clock faces for a little side jangle. Working the gears until they slid together easy.

He loved those cuckoos the best. Bastard cuckoos. Like they are just waiting for you to get comfortable and forget time is passing. You get all soft and relaxed. Forget to worry about how many hours are on your paycheck and how you can get more out of a week that's already gone. As soon as you've thought yourself light, poof, out the wall they come screaming.

I wonder if broken is inherited. But I don't know any further into our past than Daddy. My parents, both orphans, met on a train without a single ticket between them. The history of my skin and bones stops there.

"Momma, after we get married Barksdale and me are going to live down there beside his Momma and Daddy. You can come live with us."

Lenny done hopped her blue-jeaned butt up on the counter right beside my tomato biscuit. Nearly pierced her own behind with the paring knife. She's so close I can smell the sugar coming off her tongue. Barksdale done dropped her off again with a mouthful of wine and kisses and fat dreams. That reminds me. I got a bone with her for sure.

As I take the freezer door handle in my hand her mouth finally zips shut. Even though I'm not looking at her I know those deep-set eyes of hers are about to pop out her head.

She hid wine in the freezer behind my frozen corn and lima beans. She's not old enough to be drinking and knows I don't like her drinking. It busted and turned the whole inside the shade of cheap cherry.

When I opened it I heard her breathing start up again and the chatter along with it.

I cleaned her mess up already. It's like this child believes in magic. Like somehow she got away with something. The freezer must've swallowed the bottle and all its broken mess.

I wanted her to believe. Just not in her Daddy's magic.

"Barksdale done asked you to marry him?"

"We talk about it."

I pretended not to find what I was looking for and closed the freezer back up. I walked back over to her. My hips barely fit between her knees. Her hair, brown as a walnut, hung past her shoulders. I laced the giant curl framing her face in between my fingers.

"Pretty girl. Lenny, you sure are a pretty girl."

She took the collar of my dress in her hands and spread it out to my shoulders.

"Momma, we need to get you a new dress. You can't hardly even see the pattern on this one anymore. Gosh Momma, don't you want a man to do sweet things for you?"

Lord, this girl. I know my face done gone red. I can feel my gray hair curling so tight down on my scalp it's probably going white. Before I yank that curl out her head, I let it go.

"What do you know about what men do for women? How you so sure it's sweet?"

"Momma, don't you miss Daddy? Wasn't it easier when he paid the bills?"

She hopped down, turned her back to me, and traced the fake formica marble grain.

I almost couldn't hear her, "remember when he brought those hound dogs home? One for each of us?"

All four of our girls love talking about their funny daddy, the jokes he told, and the hound dogs he brought home once. They don't know he won them in a poker game right after he lost our truck. It's true what they say, it's the ones you think are happy who go through with it.

She's right about my dress. I ain't had a new one for five years, since her Daddy passed away. But new dresses didn't come easy with her Daddy around either. Wendell, Lenny's daddy, struggled more than he helped, just no one knew it.

It was five years ago. Early September rains blustered in from a storm hitting down south. They weren't hard rains. Just steady. Unforgiving of imperfect roofs and root cellar failings. Wendell used to always say, *it's a bad roof brings down a house.*

We were staying with my youngest sister, Hezzie, while her husband Frank was on another stint at the county for bootlegging. We often needed a place and it kept her from being alone if some of Frank's customers showed up.

From corner-to-corner Hezzie's place was filled with curiosities. Frank's most frequent customer paid him in rocks hand-painted with scenes of big white doctor's houses and red barns. They lined the stairs from living room to attic. Atop their enormous floor model tv, the old woman in the rocking chair kept time. Ceramic chickens and roosters and the one burro with the heavy load didn't make a peep from on top of the kitchen cabinets. And thank Jesus not a single damn cuckoo clock.

I heard Wendell settle into the stripes of the armchair as me and Hezzie drew the chicken from the grease and laid it on towels.

Wendell hadn't drank in about five months. I can't say it'd been a good five months, but it had been a dry five months. It had meant a little more money. A few more chicken legs and thighs. A breast for Lenny every now and then.

He'd been on the boat all day with his brother out fishing for crappie on the pond. He broke his streak same way he started it, drinking with his brother.

Lenny wasn't so much helping me and Hezzie in the kitchen as eating. She still don't know how to cook not one thing. See how Barksdale gets on with that if they make it that far. It was time to get to the table to eat and I shooed her off to get her Daddy. I should've known better than to send Lenny after him ever.

She always talked about seeing the credits of Ole Virginia go up on the tv screen. She never mentioned the noise. Or the hole blown right up through his middle.

Hezzie won't ever complain about scrubbing him off the wall. I won't ever talk about how if he hadn't succeeded I'd've sure enough done it for him after that. Lenny was eleven.

"Barksdale's Daddy sits at the head of the table and his Momma sits right beside him. They all hold hands and say a blessing before they eat. Everybody bows their heads. His Momma set me right beside her and passed everything to me first."

This girl didn't know everything has always been passed to her first. I ain't had a piece of breast or thigh meat since she was born sixteen years ago. Hell, since her oldest sister was born 24 years ago. Nah, I been making do sucking the piddly meat off neckbones since I was born.

"A blessing, huh? Well, you can do that here." I didn't know what the hell I was saying. I ain't never been one to pray. My sister Weeze was the religious one, Jehovah's Witness. She worried the hell out of me with all those pamphlets.

Lenny finally took a seat on the barstool. Took my cigarettes in and out of the pack. Flipped the pages of the notepad by the rotary. Twirled a pen in between her fingers. I could tell she's working up to something. Oh, that burning was climbing up my back again. I'd've thrown that damn cold biscuit in the trash if I wasn't so hungry.

"Momma, who's this?" She pulled a tiny photo from under a notepad and turned it over in her hand, "It says landlady. I don't know her."

This? I thought for sure we were going somewhere else. Maybe straight talk about that belly and this marrying stuff.

"Momma! Are you feeling alright? I keep finding this picture of this lady." Lenny sat there flapping that tiny picture of Violet so hard I felt a breeze.

A few months after me and Wendell got married—after we'd already lived in three different places—he come home and everything changed forever, "We going to Norfolk. Me and Frank got jobs."

I still have the first picture the Hoffmans, our Norfolk landlords, ever gave us—the one of Violet Hoffman that Lenny was busy smashing her fingerprint into. Wendell and Frank worked steady and honest there welding the Battleship Wisconsin. We lived in the same apartment for a whole year without ever thinking of where we'd get to next when this all fell apart. Without knowing it always falls apart.

We were all happy even if for different reasons. Wendell felt like a man cause he paid the bills and didn't nobody talk down to him. It was a noble thing welding the biggest US Naval ship there'd ever been. It was honorable to be helping our boys at war. He had a card called him a Merchant Marine.

We used to walk along the shore at night. I thought we'd be there forever. Our landlords were our dearest friends besides Frank and Hezzie. Even though Hezzie was only fourteen she'd married Frank, Wendell's best friend, and come with us. Violet Hoffman was more my age. A little older. We got on well.

Frank had Hezzie working too. Not me, Wendell was so proud to sit me down. I spent my days walking with Violet along the shore and my nights walking with Wendell. It could not have been more perfect. I have never been happier.

"Momma, why in the world are you keeping around a picture of a landlady?"

Children know few boundaries when it comes to the bodies what made them. "They were good to us. What are you jealous? I got plenty pictures of you I keep up with too."

I snatched it from her fingertips and slid it into my dress pocket. Feeling Violet's smile warm on my thumb.

"Damn Momma. You gave me a papercut."

"Don't you cuss me. And a papercut ain't gone be the worst thing you ever get."

This girl tries me.

"Momma, why are you so mad tonight?"

I picked up one of my loose cigarettes Lenny'd set rolling on the counter. Sometimes, it's best to smoke when you got nothing nice to say.

I don't guess we'd have ever come back from Norfolk if Hezzie hadn't come home early from work sick with their first son in her belly.

Forgotten as quickly as found, Lenny flung her back against the avocado refrigerator, arms flown open wide, "You can't believe how sweet she is and her skin's so soft. And her dress was so pretty and green and her eyes are just like Barksdale's, blue as glass birds. And she wore this cameo Barksdale's Daddy brought her back from World War II when he was in Italy. She wore it right here Momma."

Oh Lord Jesus, back to Barksdale's momma.

"Italy, Momma. You know where that is?"

Like I didn't live through World War II. Like I ain't never loved someone.

Even though my other girls didn't finish high school, they all just seemed to better understand whatever they were looking at then Lenny did. Each one of my sisters got at least one broken child, Lenny's mine I reckon. Broke and broken. Maybe we all are?

I rested my burning Chesterfield on an ashtray thick enough to butter the backside of a man's head when he's done wrong. Forced my foot from my shoe and rubbed the heart of my stockinged foot on the barstool rung. Rocked back and forth on the chocolate-buttercream-brown cushion trying to pay attention to my baby girl. Enjoying my hips feeling more narrow than they'd ever been with a man around. Or around a man.

"Momma, are you even listening to me at all? Barksdale's Momma's gone teach me her yeast roll recipe."

When Wendell told me where we were headed, I like to died. I'd have never thought I'd be big city. But I loved Norfolk. The way bodies created a heat that made scent just rise up from the ground. Like every breath was carrying the skin of another. And being on the beach was like being right up against the universe.

Sometimes when me and Violet went out walking if we took long enough, went far enough, she'd reach out and brush along the bony side of my arm, from my elbow to my wrist. Her small fingers would slide along my palm. Made my tongue water. A heat rise from my lower belly to my top. And we'd almost skip like silly girls holding hands. I felt so light. So small in a good way.

One day the rains came so hard it just wasn't reasonable to go for a walk. We meant to play Yahtzee. Or maybe it was Bridge. I don't know. Maybe we didn't mean to do any of that.

Cause we didn't sit at the table. We sat on the couch. We didn't have any cards or a cup or even any dice.

She reached for my cheek the same way she reached for my hand. My tongue wet and wrapped around her tiny index finger. It was just so easy to lay back for her. The way I stayed so wet as she traced my breastbone right down to my spiritual heart. The way she kissed me right there on it. Like she knew what she was doing.

My dress slid open and she traced my enormous nipples. I'd always felt so ashamed of their size and their dark color like a fruit pit. All my size. All my unexpected splotches. But I just let her see it. In the middle of the day.

It was like I heard it and didn't hear it. As though I didn't care. The clipping in the hallway. The turn of the knob. Hezzie's gasp.

"Oh Momma, I know what it is." Lenny must've exhausted herself with all the twirling. She flung herself backwards on the counter. "You won't date because you miss Daddy so much. If anything ever happens to Barksdale, I'll never date again as long as I live." And with that she flounced right on out the room.

I smashed out my cigarette, let the last exhale through my nose, and said to the kitchen, "I will tell you this, I eat the neck meat off the chicken because I damn well like it." Once Lenny finished high school, I was getting in that Galaxie and going straight east to Norfolk.

Michele Binegar
Moods of Mantis

Bonnie Proudfoot

Deer

Deer, it is for you that I write this because it is hunting season, and parked along the wide shoulders of gravel lanes are late-model pickup trucks with empty gun racks. Men with blaze orange vests and rifles, shell boxes and lunch pails lean against camper-tops or tailgates, stare at me when I run by. I keep my pace, past the last parked truck at the bend in the road, past the shotgun house sagging from subsidence and sunk into the hill where a gaunt yellow pit bull, incapable of holding more than one thought, lunges against his thick chain each time he sees me. I skirt the wide puddle where the creek spills over its banks, past the cat carcass shoved against the ditch, once recognizable by its white paws, but now just a tawny shape, its form disarranged. The road narrows. I run, and I come upon you.

Deer, last week, as I ran the paved road behind the high school, I heard a short burst, a crack, an echo, a whistle just beyond my ears. It stopped me mid-stride. My heart pummeled my ribcage. I turned, saw movement in drawn blinds on the porch of a house. I took the stairs two at a time. I didn't have a chance to knock. Two shirtless teenage boys, soft white chests, grey sweats, stood in the doorway framed in dim fluorescent kitchen light. Before I could speak, the taller one began to apologize, said he did not know it was loaded; behind him, the shorter one nodded, his eyes pale blue ping-pong balls, bobbing between his brother and me as if I am the one who has a gun, as if I have it pointed at him. They begged me not to tell their father, who I knew to be the art teacher at the high school. And I did not tell a soul, not a word. But now I tell you, Deer, browsing in a thicket of tall purple raspberry canes just beyond the creek, that they drew a bead on me, they tracked me through the sights on the barrel as I ran, that one of them pulled the trigger.

Deer, I'm not sure if you are a doe or a buck. I see a thick, shaggy white tail and tawny rump as you bound into a thicket at the brink of the woods. Deer, death comes at us. You might sense this more than I do, how you know that you must eat more because the days are cold, or how you hear my feet strike the road, my panting breath, long before I see you. And I don't have to say anything, but still I think, Run, Deer, before hunters in the woods head down to the road, and hunters on the roadside head back to the woods. Run now, while you are still strong, and I have given you a fair start.

Barbara Marie Minney

Roadblocks

The gray Northeast Ohio sky
pickets the horizon with a murky luster,
a shadowy fog obscuring the frozen lake,
a solitary great blue heron
scavenging the shore.

A solitary gentlewoman meanders
through sleeping fields
bone-crushing guillotined corn stalks,
ghosts gleaming in her eyes
exchanging fire with the murderer of her true self.

Respecting blazing memory snapshots,
never learning how to be a woman from her mother
or applying makeup,
or taking off her bra
without first removing her blouse.

We are undependable commentators
having the vaguest sense of ourselves
crafting stories that
omit inconvenient truths,
just look at any Facebook page.

The sands of the hourglass
are flowing on her womanhood
regret and sorrow lasting a lifetime,
destroying what is beautiful,
victories hidden among the casualties.

Jesus said "Love your neighbor as yourself"
but that presumes
that you love yourself
just as "Never give up on your dreams"
presumes that you have dreams.

Dreaming is for the courageous
and so is love,
if there is a heaven
why do we say "until death do us part"
at weddings?

Elizabeth Tussey

It's Got Me a Mess
—From February 16ᵗʰ, 2012 edition of The Salem News

Recent explosions in Salem Township   caused
                  suffering from Post-Traumatic Stress Disorder.

John C.   a veteran   served   auditory hallucination after one
explosion.   *I thought I was losing my mind. The far-off artillery, a few*
nights I felt them.

John   lives   Route 558,   lives through the vine, through   reports
of explosions in the township. In a million years   he heard them.
           I thought it was just me.

All   explosions at night with all but one in the township   that came
to pin-points.   Theories   range   seismic charges
nothing   fits the   thread.

John has lived: *can't begin to tell you ... a lot of the nights walked*
my house with my trying   where it's coming from.

One person who   learned the setup   is involved and   dangerous after
dark,
during daylight   a group of people was called to watch
the least exploding   on Butcher Road.
The seismic charges in   shale drilling, underground soundings for the
    drilling.

The company   specializes seismic
acquisitions and
        maps the oil and gas   The procedure requires
geo-phones along the roadside.

A representative explained
    the right-of-way,
used   up   the during daylight hours
               like exploding.

John   said *the explosions were something completely new.*
Other vets   heard it too but they live on the other side   I
don't know about the others   I can't live like this. This has got to stop.

John   looked for   but hasn't seen.
Sometimes it sounds   Other times
   on the battlefield   away.

It's got me a mess.

Elizabeth Tussey

Enter Into His Gates with Thanksgiving
—Following a photograph of Piketon
Community Church, Pike County, Ohio

Enter into His gates with thanksgiving,
with one plea: keep me among the living.

In the symmetry of the path familiar faces
flit away from the land of the living.

Despaired to death, ruin-bound
it is so hard to keep on living.

In the vacuum of future forfeit
I search for those no longer living.

Leaving the door open, I Lazarus-strut
with loves who are not living

I make the deisul, I buckle sun-wise
I carry my dead throughout my living

Enter into His Gates with Thanksgiving,
and with the grace to keep on living

Before the gates I linger, I shout
my hymn: I am not finished with my living.

Cecile Dixon

The Lord Sent a Nurse

In the spring of 2006, life was cumbersome. I was single-parenting my granddaughter, who at sixteen had morphed from a sweet little girl into a spawn of something unrecognizable. My personal life was a shambles as I was dating a married man. I really didn't want him to leave his wife, whom I didn't have any vendetta toward. But I also didn't want to spend the rest of my life waiting for the phone to ring. At the time I didn't have much energy or time to devote to a relationship so I convinced myself that it was all I needed. I'd bought a house and maintaining it was a bit more than I bargained for. Cleaning gutters, fixing water leaks and trimming hedges was much more than I'd imagined. Most weeks I was doing good just to keep the yard mowed. Add the stress of working every weekend night, as a charge nurse in a busy college town emergency department. I was a pressure cooker with a clogged vent.

I'd only had three hours sleep between my two twelve hours shifts. I woke with a lack of sleep headache and my feet began to throb before I'd set them on the floor. My granddaughter had wrecked her hand me down car the previous week. I hadn't finished my evening wake-up ritual of Mountain Dew and Marlboro, when she began begging to drive my car that night. I said no on principal.

"But Nana, you'll be at work. You don't need it. I'll pick you up in the morning when your shift is over," she begged.

"No. You wrecked your car," I reminded her.

"That wasn't my fault."

"That's not what the police said." It went on like that, tit for tat until, against my better judgment, she wore me down and I gave in.

When she dropped me off at work. She said, "I'll see you at six."

I didn't answer. I trudged inside, the warning valve on my pressure cooker clanging away.

Inside the ED (emergency department) business was as usual. Saturday night had started early. There were a couple drunken students already sleeping it off in a couple beds. Although the patients complained about the ED being cold, I was sweating. Irritation bubbled under my skin. I tried to ignore it. The ED was short staffed and I was teaching a nursing student. The Doc was frustrated and taking it out on everyone, ordering unecessary tests and procedures. Every order got the staff further behind. Patients complained about the wait. The nursing student asked a million questions. I debated calling the Doc outside, to show him reason or to hit him. I wasn't sure which.

Around eleven, the Doc ordered yet another unnecessary cath urine on a fully functional ambulatory female. The camel's back broke. I had to get out of there. It wasn't a choice. I had to leave. I first called my granddaughter and told her to bring my car back. My tone must have said, 'no argument' because she didn't.

Then I called my nursing supervisor: "I'm leaving you have to come in."

"I'm not coming in and you can't leave…it's patient abandonment. You'll lose your license," she said.

"That's why I called you, I have to leave." Fifteen minutes later when she walked in to the ED, her eyes puffy with sleep, I walked out the door without a word.

My granddaughter was waiting in the employee parking lot and I nodded my head for her to let me drive. I didn't know what I was going to do. I just knew that I never wanted to be a nurse again. I never wanted to parent or be a grandmother again. I wasn't sure if I even wanted to exist anymore.

Silently, I drove home. I pulled to the curb in front of the house and waited until the granddaughter climbed out. She paused with the door open and gave me a look that said, "What are you going to do?" I didn't answer. When she closed the door, I drove away.

I got onto the highway heading south. I drove, not having any plan or reason for my direction. The road was mostly deserted with headlights of a few trucks. I drove fast and reckless through the darkness, sometimes crying with frustration and sometimes pounding the wheel in anger. Muscle memory steered the car.

I'd been driving for a while, when I rounded a bend and saw odd looking lights about a half mile up ahead. I slowed down and drove with a caution that I hadn't been using. The off kilter lights looked like a UFO landed there in the middle of I-75.

As I got closer I could make out that it was a jack-knifed eighteen-wheeler. The reason the lights looked so alien was that the cab of the truck was on its side. The trailer was twisted in the opposite direction. The trailer's doors had ripped open and the highway was littered with cardboard boxes. I slowed to a crawl and put on my emergency flashers.

I stopped about twenty yards from the twisted truck and parked on the side with my headlights shining on the wreck. Stepping over pieces of twisted metal I made my way to the truck's cab. The windshield was shattered and dangling in great pieces of safety glass.

"Hey," I yelled, "are you alright?" No answer so I repeated as loud as I could. "Can you hear me?"

I heard a groan. I pulled my cell from my pocket and punched 911.

"911, what's your emergency?" Came the dispatcher's voice.

"I'm at I-75 southbound, mile marker 147 and there's an overturned eighteen wheeler. The driver is alive and in the cab." After the dispatcher asked a few more questions, she told me that she was sending and ambulance and a KSP. I assured her I'd stay until help arrived.

When we disconnected I made my way back to the truck. By standing on the front tire I could pull myself up to the driver's window. By the dim dashboard lights I could see the driver was folded up under the steering wheel, bleeding from a gash in his forehead. His right leg seemed to be bent at an odd angle. "Hey buddy, I called for help, an ambulance is on the way." He didn't answer but his eyes followed the sound of my voice.

I pulled a wad of gauze out of my scrub pocket and dabbed at the blood on the man's face. "My name is Cecile, I'll stay with you until help gets here."

He groaned as I wiped the blood from his eyes. "What happened?" He croaked.

"I don't know. Appears you had a wreck, but I didn't see it." In the distance I could hear the faint whine of sirens. "Help will be here soon. What's your name?" I asked to keep him talking.

"Joe. Joe Jones."

"Where are you from, Joe?" I could now see the strobing of emergency lights rounding the curve.

"Mountain Home, Arkansas." His voice seemed stronger, more alert. A police car came to a stop behind my car and an ambulance followed. "Joe, the police and ambulance are here. I've got to get my car out of their way. They'll take good care of you now."

"Thank you," he said. I squeezed his shoulder before I hopped off the tire.

A tall KSP was standing at the edge of the road shining a flashlight on the wreckage and I walked toward him. "Were you involved in the crash?" He asked, shining his light on me.

I blinked at the light and said, "No, it must have just happened when I came upon it."

Three paramedics jumped out of the ambulance.

One medic asked me, "Are you injured?"

"No, just the truck driver. He's trapped, head injury and he might have a femur fracture." They hurried to the wrecked truck, one climbed through the window and the other two began working to get the door open.

I turned to the officer and said, "His name is Joe Jones and he said he's from Mountain Home, Arkansas. If you don't need me for anything I'll be on my way." After I showed the officer my license and he jotted down some details, I climbed back in my car and left the flashing lights in my rear view mirror.

Several more miles down the highway I saw an all night gas station and I exited the highway and pulled up to the gas pumps. After I'd filled the tank I went inside. In the restroom, as I washed my hands, I stared at my reflection. I looked old, much older than my forty-six years.

I grabbed a Mountain Dew from the cooler and set it on the counter. "Is that all?" the tattooed, clerk asked.

"Give me two packs of Marlboro Ultra Lights," I answered.

He rang up the gas, soda and cigarettes. "You on your way to work?" he asked. I must have looked confused because he nodded to the nametag dangling around my neck.

I grunted a noncommittal response, paid and left before he tried to start a conversation about the noble profession of nursing. Lighting a cigarette, I pulled the car back onto the highway. My fugue returned. I didn't notice when I passed the exit for my hometown. I didn't notice when I passed the exit for my alma mater or the place we'd vacationed when I was a child. I drove on through the darkness, lost in thought, trying to mentally undo all the wrong decisions I'd made.

Through my foggy brain I saw the exit for the Oneida, Kentucky tunnel to Tennessee. I braked and almost slid off the road trying to steer to the ramp. Nothing seemed more important than watching the sun come up from the Cumberland Gap Overlook.

The lookout was much farther than I'd estimated and the winding, two lane road made driving much slower. By the time I arrived there the sun was coming up and my burning eyes couldn't see the beauty I'd been hoping to find. Too tired to drive further, I parked my car in a shady spot, lowered my windows and closed my eyes. I fell asleep quick and hard.

I don't know how long I'd been there before a, "tap, tap, tap," by my head woke me. I opened my eyes to find a park ranger bent with his face in the open window.

"Mam, are you alright?" he asked.

I shook my head and brushed the sleep from my eyes with my hands. "Yeah I'm fine," I answered. "I've been driving most of the night and I just wanted to get a nap."

"Can I see your license?" he asked.

For the second time that night I handed my driver's license to an officer. I watched as he carried them to his patrol car and spoke into a radio mic. Then he jotted down some things on a paper clipped to a clipboard. After speaking into the mic for a second time he walked back to my window.

"Mam, you can't sleep in the park. Only designated campgrounds and those are reserved months ahead. This is for your safety." He handed my license back.

"Yes I understand."

"The closet accommodations for sleeping are on the Kentucky side of the tunnel. Drive safe and get some rest," he said before walking back to his car, making a wide U-turn and leaving the parking lot.

I sighed and drank the last of the hot Mountain Dew left from the night before. The park ranger was parked across the road. I nodded a thank you and retraced my path.

Once back on the Kentucky side of the tunnel, I saw two familiar signs, Walmart and McDonalds. The scrubs I was wearing were clinging to my skin and smelled. I decided I'd visit Wal-Mart first. Inside the store I grabbed a cheap t-shirt and shorts, toothbrush, paste and deodorant. Next I headed to McDonalds. I figured on using their restroom to change clothes and freshen up some. Then I could mull my next move over French fries and a large Diet Coke.

When I pushed the restroom door open, the first thing that caught my eye were two neatly dressed, little gray haired ladies in the open door of the handicapped stall. They were frantically gesturing, their eyes tearful. I moved past a McDonald's employee to get a look at what they were so upset about.

Wedged between the commode and the bathroom wall was a tiny fragile looking woman. She looked to be around the same age as the two standing in the doorway. Under her shoulder was a wadded up knit hat. The harsh bathroom light glared off her bald, head and her lack of eyelashes and eyebrows cried out chemo.

"They can't get her up off the floor," the McDonald's employee said in my direction. "I told them the only thing I could do was call an ambulance."

I ignored her and asked the little ladies guarding the door if I could help. "Oh please yes," they said.

I made my way into the crowded stall and squatted by the woman. "Are you injured? Do you want me to call an ambulance?"

"No I'm not hurt, I just slid off the commode." She paused, and caught her breath before continuing, "This happens, that's why I've been down here staying with my sisters so they could look after me."

"Do you want me to help you up?" I asked.

"Oh yes please." All three women answered in unison.

"Can you both please step back?" I said to the sisters. And to the McDonald's employee I asked, "Can you push her wheelchair into the doorway?"

Once the wheelchair was in place with its wheels locked, I asked, "Is it ok if I touch you?"

She nodded yes, weakly.

I put my hands under her armpits and lifted her fragile body to a standing position before pivoting her and placing her in the wheelchair as gently as possible. After I'd placed her feet on the footpads I pushed her into the restaurant. Her sisters followed.

The McDonald's employee held the knit hat out to the woman, saying, "My break is over. I got to get back to work."

The lady tugged the hat over her bald scalp and all three thanked her.

"Where are y'all headed?" I asked.

"To Lexington," one women said. "Sara has an appointment there." She nodded at the fragile woman in the wheelchair.

"At the Markie Women's Center," the other sister chimed in, then leaned close to me and added in a lowered voice, "Her cancer is back."

"I'm just so tired, I don't think I can sit up in that car another two hours," Sara said and rested her head on her arm.

"If we call an ambulance they'll take you to the nearest emergency department," I said.

"No, no, no," all three sisters said.

"I'm going to Markie for end of life care," Sara said weakly, "They've done all they can and," she paused, "I'm ready to go."

Both sisters sniffed sadly and looked away.

Some good meaning soul must have called 911, for at that moment two uniformed paramedics entered the door and scanned the dining area until their eyes found us. "Oh please," Sara cried softly," If they take me to a hospital the doctors will insist on doing all kinds of tests. I've already had all the tests over and over. Please don't let them take me."

I stood and placed myself between the medics and the ladies. I quickly explained the situation to the young men.

"You're right," they agreed, "we can only transport to the nearest hospital." The older of the two then said, "But Rural Metro can take her to Lexington."

I was familiar with the chain medical transport company. "Do you have the local number?" I asked, pulling out my cell.

They gave me the number and I punched it in my phone. A compassionate dispatcher listened as I explained the situation. She asked for insurance information. One of the sister's gave me Sara's Medicare card and I relayed it to the dispatcher.

After about ten minutes she came back with, "Yes we can take her, but we need a name of an accepting person at Markie."

"I'll work on that." I hung up and asked the sisters if they had a number for The Markie Center. They did and I dialed it. When someone answered I again explained Sara's plight.

"Oh my, we were getting worried about Sara. We were expecting her a couple hours ago."

I sighed a sigh of relief and the person on the other end said, "Let me connect you to the house supervisor, Marilyn.

Within minutes Marilyn agreed to phone Rural Metro. One of the paramedics brought us all rounds of drinks courtesy of McDonalds. The other medic moved their ambulance. They wanted to stay and make sure the ladies got the help they needed. Before we'd finished our drinks, a Rural Metro Ambulance pulled up to the curb. They efficiently brought in a gurney and helped a pale Sara lay down. As they took her vitals I patted her on the shoulder and wished her well. When they wheeled her out the entire restaurant, staff and customers applauded. Sara waved her pale hand, like a queen in her chariot.

After the Rural Metro ambulance left, I walked the sisters to their car. "Now y'all drive slow. They're gonna get there way before you," I cautioned.

The older sister asked, "Can I hug you?"

"I never turn down a hug," I said and wrapped my arms around her tiny body. The hug was a healing touch for me. I was so very tired, but a good tired now and her hug gave me a warm peace.

The sister pulled back and touched my cheek. "We were in that bathroom praying for help and the good Lord sent a nurse." She slid behind the wheel and slowly maneuvered her big sedan from the parking lot.

I stood there, still in my sweaty scrubs, feeling better about myself than I had in weeks. I was a nurse. It didn't matter if I was in a busy emergency room on the clock or at the scene of a wreck or even in McDonald's restroom. I was a nurse.

I said my thank you's to everyone. Rounded up the bag with my toiletries, went back in the restroom, freshened up, changed clothes. Then I called my boss. When she answered, I said, "Hey, have I still got a job?"

Teresa Sager
Appalachian Campfire

Sarah Diamond Burroway

October: Our Lady, post-ICU

She used to hold my hand when we were waiting
For time to get out of bed. For the bus.
For dad to get home from work.
In times unsure, her fingers locked with mine
gave me strength to face shadows and monsters under the bed.

I trusted her mastery of clocks: their twisted hands to me, a mystery.
Unsure of their arrowed arms jutting in unending swirls-
stroking numbers just above the jawbones of flat, white faces.
It is hard to know if there's just a little left or maybe so much left to hold onto.
How do you know what to do when time spins so fast?

My heart wants to run but I stay
and look for angels in the corners of this sterile room.
I want to turn back the dial to a time
when clocks ticked more slowly.
She rests behind a hush of doors- screens flashing, devices beeping.

Their soundtrack signals we are still here.
I don't know what to say or what time it is
so, I pull my chair close and hold her hand
like she used to hold mine.
Together, unhurried.

Sarah Diamond Burroway

Places in Between

Between her room and Genevieve's (is that her name?)
is a shared bathroom, unused.
Clean, the scent of institutional mops and chlorine,
two bedpans the color of marigolds sit idly beside a retro-toilet-
a throne with a cushioned lift to help old knees, now, unable to bend.
The tiled floor is grayed white, like November.
Walls, gridded squares mocking with their orderly array.
Nothing here is predictable. Yet, everything is the same.
If dinge had a color, this would be it.
I step away from my mother's bed,
guided by the shimmer of a network sitcom.
Inside, I pull the door behind me
then check the door to Genevieve's room and latch it.

This is the quiet moment, away from moans and pain

The sting of tears in jaundiced eyes.
My own gaze now a blur, jaw clenched against emotion.
I hear the woman on the other side cry out to a memory-child.
Her baby roams the fields of her mind,
playing in the shade of trees
with glints of sunlight dancing on the grass,
tickling toes that have lost their shoes.
I lean toward my mother's door, bend to hear if she is stirring.
My chest pulls in, muscles muzzle a sob-
throat tightens to lock in my cries.
Silence. Mine and hers.
Heartstrings that want to pull back, tether down, hold tight?
No words can say what this is, a place of passage to another world.

Can you go all the way to the end and not feel that?

Genevieve lulls into a slumbered hush, then a slight snore.
Temporary relief from pain and fear,
soft faced like a sleeping baby.
I hear my mother calling for her own mother
like a child, unsure.

Mother, mother, mother…
scripting again and again.
Nothing I can do is enough.
Mother, mother, this is all I can give.
"Shh, I'm here now. I'm here."

Sarah Diamond Burroway

The brochure did not adequately prepare me | 12-3-2017

Pursed and hard,
lips reject
food needed to sustain
her healing,
      spewed, snubbed, unwanted.
No extreme measures.
Harsh wishes
must be observed,
carried out by those left behind.
Those already grieving, those who are angry
      that time is running short.
These are the final days
And I am not ready
for goodbye.
Power of attorney can't control
      the inevitable verdict.
Power of attorney
can only influence the impact,
call for chemical relief at 6 and 12
to ease the parting,
      the harsh separation from life, from breath.

No conversation
for focus.
Eyes clouded,
ears muffled,
mouth, still and quiet.
Hush.
Don't cry.
She is done.

She is done with the emotion of now.

Catherine Pritchard Childress

Cirrhotic

Sometimes the dead need to hear death's process:

1. *Fluid will accumulate in your abdomen. This can be uncomfortable and cause difficulty breathing.* Check.

Sometimes the dead laugh and tell you if you have anything wonderful to say about them you should say it now, but you only think of their skinny ankles and calves, the green Hornet they drove to the pool—your cousins piled inside, even the one who dry-humped you upstairs when you were eight and believed it was a game.

Sometimes they are lying in living rooms in hospital beds delivered by Hospice waiting for the doctor's pronouncement; aware of every pouched micturition, every defecation, conscious others are too, but too polite to acknowledge the shittiness.

2. *As the liver loses its ability to detoxify, harmful chemicals build up in the blood and brain, leading to mental changes.* Check.

3. *As brain function continues to decrease, sleep and confusion will increase.* Check

4. *The doctor may prescribe medications to help maintain comfort and dignity.*

Sometimes the dead think their favorite aqua blouse too ordinary for burial, that caskets should be open because "people will be curious." Sometimes they count seconds between abdominal cramps.

5. *In the final days of liver failure, medication will be less useful.* Check

6. "Please God, come take me now." Check.

Catherine Pritchard Childress

Sōkhenet

". . .Let us look for a young virgin to serve the king
and take care of him. She can lie beside him
so that our lord the king may keep warm." —I Kings 1:4

Prescribed for my virtue, beauty,
promise I can restore this man,
his impotent fields, the kingdom
bound in his vigor. No small task—
its weight bearing down like quilts
heaped high on his withering frame.

So cold he resists wool's comfort
yet finds in my body a balm,
respite from sure surrender—
to his wife, his sons,
his deteriorating flesh.
Still, no one body, however

servile, however pure can meet
the needs of a king. Even when
his pulse quickens beneath my touch
I know what those who brought me here—
counselors, physicians, greedy
sons—do not. I am not enough.

Catherine Pritchard Childress

Capriccio

Through the kitchen window I see ropes
swinging from the maple's arthritic limb
then the lengthening fingers of the maestro
conducting her strings in a concerto,
each grip cueing another turn that spirals her,
summer-knotted hair skimming the grass,
upturned face scored by sun and leaf shadow,
bare feet raised toward the whirling cord
that winds *ritardando* to a breathtaking end.

Donna Weems

The Storm (Song)

Chorus:
I stand here, my face lifted to the rain,
close my eyes, nothing is the same.
Mingled with the rain are tears.
It's the dark storm and hidden fears,
that numb the heart, break us apart,
where do we start, where do we start, where do we start again, from
here?

You came with a tractor and a dog,
wielding tools and some slim dialogue.
You could mend the fences,
lose false pretenses,
you found the heart of my ways,
how to turn hours into days.
Chorus

The fields are plowed and planted with grain.
You have wandered, but you still remain.
You do the chores;
pack winter's stores.
What is the trouble in your head?
Only the dog sleeps in my bed.
Chorus

Your words build walls in our lives.
Your anger brings nothing but strife.
I am lost at home.
With you I am alone.
Don't make me pay for your past.
Leave it behind, so our love will last.
Chorus

Donna Weems

Spirit of the Forest (Song)

A fairy lived among the children
dancing in their laughter
lighting up their smiles
she loved the children dearly
and kept pace with them awhile.

She showed them the forest
lit a path for wandering feet
they found wonder
in the waters
of the clear and gamboling creek.

Oh, children let me see your smiles.
Oh, children stay with me awhile.

The birds were all a twitter
when the fairy
called them down
from the highest branches
to perch on the ground.

Soon fairy, birds, and children
sang for all to hear.
The forest
rang with music
whenever they were near.

Oh, warblers what company you bring!
Oh, thrushes teach us how to sing.

With the fairy's guidance
the children became wise.
Wild creatures
learned to trust them
without trickery or guise.

Oh, little cottontail let me pet your fur.
Oh, wild kittens I want to hear your purr.

But fairies ne'er grow old
as children want to do.
They found families,
jobs, and hobbies—
a larger field of view.

Wherever life
will lead them
they will not forget
the spirit of the forest
lies deep within their breasts.

Oh, children let me see your smiles.
Oh, children stay with me awhile.

Marlene L'Abbé
Girl With Wool Roving

Pauletta Hansel

Biography of My Breasts

Left breast, right breast you don't remember growing,
but you do remember going to the dress shop
on Main —measure, prod and pack them
in with straps and cups, and aren't you just
a big girl now,
big pink hips and thighs and belly, little
breasts that push against the fabric
of your body, aren't you a little
old to play wrestle with the boys?

***

Left breast,
right breast, that's the one
that's bigger, coned cup tipping
pink nipple down.
Remember, if you can hold a pencil
underneath your breast, that means you
have to work a little harder, be a little
smaller girl; I mean, you're old
enough to starve away,
erase the contours of the right breast
pouring out its perkiness. Girl, you gotta
let that pencil fall.

***

Cringe and flinch at memory
you don't want,
that handsome doctor hovering
up above your left breast, right breast,
have your nipples always
been inverted? and you say,
trying perky on like a pink paper gown,
not when they've grown hard.

***

Flattened into round steak
on a tray—breathe in, now hold
left breast, then right
pressed inside that cold contraption,
is there something
pink and hard you don't remember
growing deep inside?

***

…and in your life
you don't remember anybody but the one
who loves you now, and later,
who ever touched so sweetly
left breast, right breast,
one and then the other.
Pink cupped tongue.

Pauletta Hansel

Poem Written While Contemplating
a Newly Dug Southern Kentucky Grave

Neither born nor buried in such bright, heavy earth,
my mother, in between,
found a patch of her own and claimed it,
tamed it with horse shit and other black offerings
night after night as the sun went down behind a rise
so gentle she would hardly call it a hill,
much less a mountain. She knew
her mountains.
The shadows they made.
Here, only hers bent and rose, bent again
to make the bed her lilies would rise from.
Come fall she would press her small foot hard
against the spade's square edge,
push it deep through the layers of soil
to fling at my feet a pale, dangled cluster
I carried north, clay still clinging
to the roots. My mother
is ash now, her garden mowed over
and sown with someone else's seed.
By my door her lilies,
streaked red as turned clay.

Dana Wildsmith

Listen

"I got me eleven acres out to Homer. Don't nobody know I'm there. That's the way I like it. Got a creek as wide as this road."

The man shifts to neutral and eases his sweaty back to the orange leather driver's seat of a county road-grader. He's older than me, but not by much; I'd bet good money he was born right at the tail end of the Baby Boom, just like me. I've got a lot more hair left on my head than he does, but he's got me beat when it comes to stomach size. I'm happy about both those facts. I can't tell how we'd measure up height-wise because his perch puts him ten feet over the road right now, so he's talking down to me, but only in a literal sense.

He swipes a bandana across his forehead and then gives it a wave my direction to make sure I'm paying him mind.

"I built a little cabin right on that creek for me and my wife to live in while I built a house. You know what she said? Said she wasn't movin'. Wanted to stay right in that cabin."

We both look down the southernmost end of Harry McCarty Road as if we could see his wife's little cabin sitting there where my road ends, instead of Clarence Edwards' old tenant house standing empty like it has for a couple of decades now.

Yep, and now I see one more thing that needs noticing—I give Mama's cat a yell.

"Peter! Get out of the road before a truck runs you over."

Mama's lazy grey favorite doesn't even raise his head from the cool sand. Peter's an old soul, born at one with his North Georgia farm.

"Aw, leave him lay." The man presses his lips tight together in a straightwise smile, but his eyes go gentle. "He'll move fast enough, 'fore a car gets to him."

The man's smile goes soft as his eyes.

"Nothin' I like better than a big-headed old tom cat."

Peter stretches out his handsome legs in a mighty act of exertion, then spreads himself even flatter on the road, save for the hump of his belly mounding like a second white hill on this highest rise of my white sand road.

The County man's watching Pete, too.

"Now see? See right there where your mama's cat's at? That's natural drainage. This road of yours drains dry after a rain, always has done. No need to scrape and bring in dirt and gravel—just messes up what don't need fixing. God got it right the first time."

He hangs his arm longer out the cab window and winks.

"Now that's just between you and me, hear? Far as the County's concerned, I scrape this part of the road twice a year, don't I, now?"

I grin and jerk my head once in a nod of affirmation, *Yessir,* and then we both just mull for a minute.

It feels good to stand and let the sweat dry. I'm resting my weight against my hoe, rocking just a little. I nod at him again, to say we understand each other.

You'd think to look at us we'd known each other long and well, and we have, in the way of neighbors passing and nodding day after day, but I don't have a clue what his name is. Never has seemed to matter. He's the County Man, and I'm that girl whose preacher daddy bought the old Edwards place thirty years back. My roots go just thirty years deep, but he's seen enough of me and my family working this land to care that nothing bad happens to us.

The man looks at me and shakes his head the way a man does when he can't understand why a woman does what she does, but it sure does tickle him.

"You don't never get afraid out here on this road all by yourself but for your mama, do you?"

I smile, and shrug, then have to quick catch my hoe when it slips from my shoulder.

"I don't guess so. Maybe a little nervous sometimes. Every now and then we get a kind of creepy sort out here."

"Creepy?"

He doesn't like that at all. His face goes hard and narrow.

"Well, like the guy the other week who came walking by real fast carrying a pickax and a bucket."

"What'd he look like?"

"Oh, I don't know. Dirty blond hair and beard."

I look up at the County man from under my eyebrows and smile.

"And I mean *dirty.*"

He smiles, too, glad of a reason to.

"Old-youngish," I go on, "maybe mid-thirties. Sharp nose. Looked like he could've played second-string football in high school. It wasn't so much how he looked as what he said. When I asked him what was up, he told me he was going to dig for gold on Harrison's land. *I got permission,* he told me."

I roll my eyes the way Mama hates, but the County man doesn't seem to get how weird this whole encounter was. I hold my hands out, palms up and try again.

"The guy believed he was going to find gold? That was what was creepy."

The road man's nodding his head, but not like he's agreeing with me

"I know who you're talking about. That boy's messed up, but he ain't crazy."

The sun's out hotter now. It's getting on toward noon. He pulls the bandana from his shirt pocket again and wipes it twice across his forehead, swiping all the way across in one direction, then back again.

"Honey," he says while he refolds the bandana and tucks it back," you know there's gold in Georgia's hills, don't you?"

"Well, yeah, but that's up near Dahlonega, not here. And besides, that was mostly all mined out a century ago. All we have now is Fool's Gold washing up along the creek banks."

"Nah, girlee, that's not exactly so."

Peter rouses himself from the road where the sand's getting too hot for napping. He saunters past the big machine resting dead center on his road, letting his tail drag lightly along the grader's mammoth wheels as he passes. The man reaches down from the cab's window and wiggles his fingers, air-scratching Peter's proud spine.

"See, one summer when I was a kid, I was up at my granddaddy's farm in Canton, helping him yank up rotted fence posts and set new ones. This one old post, when it come up, it kind of glinted all over, like gold. My granddaddy, he told me it *was* gold. He told me how that gold they dug way back then is still in our hills, just not so much. My granddaddy said sometimes when there's been a spring of heavy rain, little flecks of gold can wash down through loose soil, and it can go a long ways, he told me, until it catches hold on something like that old fence post with holes rotted all over it."

Hmm. I'm thinking this over when I see Mama come out on her side porch. She's wondering why the road scraper's been sitting so long on our road. It can't be for a good reason, she's thinking to herself. County visitations never are.

So I wave: *It's okay, Mama! Just talking!*

The man waves, too.

"Your mama's a good woman."

I know.

I look up at him again.

"So you're telling me this guy really was digging for gold? Mr. Harrison really gave him permission to root around in his cow pastures?"

"I'm sayin' Mr. Harrison has knowed that boy's family since before that boy was born. Mr. Harrison knows any baby born to that family don't have an ice cube's chance in hell of ever comin' out on the winnin' side of life. *What harm's it gonna do*, Mr. Harrison probably asked hisself, *to let the boy spend his afternoons looking for gold in my fields? Better he should do that, than cook meth in one a my old chicken houses.*"

Now I'm feeling a little bit ashamed, but not too much. The guy was creepy; I stand by that.

I shift my hoe to my other hand and lean toward the north for a bit. The County man nods at my hoe, and then looks behind me to where I've left my wheelbarrow standing, my shovel resting upside-down in the wheelbarrow's bed.

"My wife's doing the same thing as you, laying down mulch between the rows in her garden. When the rain stops, come July, her beans won't fry up and neither will yours cause that mulch'll hold the rain in. And mulch ain't nothing but dirt that ain't broken down yet, so it'll go right back into your garden dirt and make it better."

I turn to look at my wheelbarrow, swiveling the hoe with me as I turn. It was Daddy's wheelbarrow; that's why I keep using it, old and dented and cement-pocked as it is. I like tools with a history to them.

I turn back around to the man.

"Were you around when Buddy used to keep a still in my woods?"

It's obvious he was, because he's already nodding his head and grinning.

"Yep, yep."

His head goes down, then up, with each *yep*. He leans a little more out the cab window and starts his story.

"I wasn't no more than twenty, just started working for the County. I'd be driving my rig along these roads and have to slow way down 'cause here'd be Buddy, pushing his wheelbarrow loaded down with sugar, right down the middle of the road. Wouldn't move over to let me by, neither. Just kept pushin' that loaded barrow like he was an honest farmer."

The man tilts his head to one side and back up again.

"I can't say as I'd of called him a farmer, but I guess he was honest. Didn't ever try to hide what he was trundling. Guess he knew we all knew where he was headin', and what he had in mind to do there, so why bother hidin'?"

What he's saying gives me back my own memories of watching Buddy and his wheelbarrow on their rounds. I crane my head to look around the grader at Mama's front porch.

"I remember many an afternoon, swinging right up there with my baby on my lap when Buddy passed by."

The man huffs out a sigh.

"Honey, I gotta tell you now, I think I'd much ruther see some guy heading into the woods to tend his still, than brewing up meth in one of those old chicken houses along Briscoe Mill. That meth is bad, real bad."

I know. One morning a few years back, I leashed my big dog Fred, grabbed my cell phone and headed into my neighbor's woods to flush out a pack of meth heads from Richard's abandoned old singlewide that sits all crack-roofed and rotting just out of sight of cars passing on my road. Seven scrawny, wild-eyed crazies came tearing past me and Fred, throwing their scabby arms over their faces to keep me from taking their pictures.

I don't tell this to the kind County man. It would worry him

"What's your wife growing in her garden this year?"

He brightens right up; I'm not sure if it's because of the garden or her. Probably it's both.

"Oh, girlee, she's planted a mort of everything, just like you, I bet. She likes the early stuff like lettuce and those little English peas. I tell her, *Hon, those don't hardly pay the rent. They come and go too quick!* But I'm just teasin' her. Anything that lady grows is good for eatin'. "

He leans out his window a little and points one finger at me, narrowing his eyes and wrinkling up his nose so I'll know now it's me he's teasing.

"The good stuff comes later. All the corn and fat old cukes and butter beans and big Yukon Gold potatoes. That's man's food."

I smile and nod my head. We understand each other.

He asks me, kind of worried, "Your mama used to keep that garden, didn't she?"

"Uh huh. It got to be too much for her when Daddy was dying. When I moved back here, I took over for her, but first I had to cut down twelve foot pines out of the garden; they grew up that quick."

"But I'll wager the soil was loamy where them pine roots was. God always leaves us a bonus for hard work. Your daddy, he was hard worker, but a good man to stop and visit. He'd be draggin' six-by-eights across this road here, just draggin' 'em by hand, not even hookin' 'em to a come-along, and he'd drop the one he was haulin' to shake my hand. Always shook my hand, dusty as I was."

The man's eyes go wet the way I've many times seen a country man's eyes look at a funeral or a birthing.

"He'd be proud to see you working his land like this."

The road man sits up from the cab's seat to push his hands flat against the small of his back.

"Girlee, I gotta get movin'. Get yourself on back out to your garden before this sun drives you in. My wife, she's doing like you this morning, tendin' her vegetables. I can't hardly get her out of the garden. She'll stay there all day, just like you, looking like it's the only place in this world she wants to be."

I nod my head, once. *Yep.*

I toss my hoe into Daddy's wheelbarrow and head to the mulch pile for another load.

The County man cranks up his rig and rumbles away, the grader's scraping blade raised high and useless all along my family's stretch of Harry McCarty Road.

Mary Beth Whitley
Sticks

Barbara Sabol

Next to me

at the flood museum, a young girl presses a button
on the diorama again, and again the mountain lake overflows
the dam, masses and rushes down the winding spine
of the Conemaugh Valley.

She scurries to keep pace with the blinking lights
along the length of the glass case as together we watch
the water gather, surge, crash into the miniature city,

then she skips back and reaches for the button, giggling
louder than the disembodied narrator. But in my head
only echoes of the wave's roar, smash of bricks and beams,
shingles ripping. Screams. Silence.

This old stone building was once a library,
my childhood haven. Weathered spines held the promise
of some incredible elsewhere while the heady blend
of Pine Sol and inked vellum in the shushed reading room
instilled the thrall of story, character, outcome.

Now I've returned to sift through artifacts—
a pair of wire spectacles (what books were read
through these lenses?), a once-white cotton glove
(folded into the other at church?), a ceramic doll
with all her limbs (what of the child who loved her?)

As I handle the sleight heft of each, the lure of story
draws me again. Sorting through boxes of musty letters
and photos, I search for a way to tell the story
of how a doll in gingham came to rest in a small pine box
in the back room of a museum.

Barbara Sabol

Waterwheel
—*Johnstown, PA. July 19, 1977*

I heard my father's story a full two days later
after frantic calls home. All wires down.
Red Cross lines besieged. *Try again later. . .*

         later.

On his way to work at the mill that morning
my father's car headed down into the city
as the flood rose to meet him, rising fast, up

the steep road so that he threw the car into reverse
and sped some one thousand feet back up that incline,
shimmying curb-to-curb all the way to the house

on Bluff Street where he woke my mother, and together
they ran to the corner, Mom still in her bathrobe, to witness
the neighborhood below become a fast-running creek.

From a collision of thunder up near Erie, a series of storms
had followed one another like train cars on a track
moving down to the Conemaugh Valley,

opening their colossal cargo of rain over our town,
bursting dams that checked the river, washing away houses,
lives. Seventy-eight souls.

Through the years he'd tell it exactly the same way,
like a passage he'd memorized for school, with the same
wide-eyed astonishment as if he were once again

watching that torrent rush toward him—trapped
behind the wheel with no option but to hightail it
backward to higher ground.

I would often ask, *tell me again, Dad, how you escaped
the flood that day*, and silently recite the story along with him,
like a prayer, and together we'd see the sky as a sheet
of molten steel, and the marvel of that surging tide.

Melissa Helton

Good Lord Willing And

The creek is rising today—
      muddy brown roar,
            branches,
            basketballs,
            Mt. Dew bottles of tobacco spit
                riding the churning current past.
The power is out and torrents
      blasting down mountainsides
         leap off cliff edges and road cuts.
      Ditches are glutted,
            tadpoles swept down toward the confluence,
            the corn planted yesterday
            a loss.
Plastic Walmart bags snag in the river weeds
      like ghost decoration in mid-November,
            out of place and out of time.
                The sky cracks open again,
     our bridge's already underwater,
       us stranded all weekend.
That's ok. We got nowhere to go.
                Everything will be scoured fresh
         tomorrow,
      the metallic flood water smell
         mixing with thick lilac and sugary katsura.

You've been gone a year and a half.
        I don't wish you were here, but I'd like you to see
           this flood.

Melissa Helton

The Adages of the Poet

If the poet drops a cup of hot coffee and the cup breaks,
expect an elder to soon tell a shocking secret.

If the poet drops a cup of hot coffee and the cup doesn't break,
expect a new baby in the family within a year.

If the poet has sudden tooth pain during the gibbous moon,
there will be a heartache.

As the dogwoods are losing their blooms, beware the poet
who chops off long hair. The venom is sharp.

As the blackberries fatten, beware the poet who studies
a foreign language. The skin is worn too thin.

The parents of poets should be wary.

If the poet lives in a state that begins with a vowel,
years ending in 5 will be lucky.

If the poet lives in a state that begins with New,
what is old should be cherished.

When the poet asks for your opinion,
tiptoe with both eyes open.

The poet who stops suddenly in the grocery aisle,
eyes unfocused beside the pickle jars,
knows the reason for your sadness.

The poet who doesn't write it down commits fraud.

The poet who writes it down commits fraud.

Melissa Helton

Momma Says

This place is lit up like a Polish church
when every light in the house is on,
especially when the bright rooms are devoid of people.

Momma says

God bless America!
when she doesn't want to say *Jesus H Christ!*
or the equivalent in frustration or exasperation.

Momma says

You fly, I'll buy
when she wants Chinese take-out and is assigning
you to drive across town with her debit card to get it.

Momma says

They couldn't organize an orgy in a whorehouse
when something that should be easy to accomplish
is being clusterfucked into debacle.

Momma says

There are certain things you don't tell your mother
when conversation is approaching
something she doesn't want to know.

Momma says

Wow, your hair is dark
and *let's not talk about unpleasant things*
and *take some money out of the account*
for your fundraiser.

Momma says

This goddamned cat! real shrill
in your ear when you're on the phone,

and *well, anyway I just called to say hello.*

Momma says

Don't change your name
and *I love you*
and *this is me being proud of you.*

Tamara M. Baxter

The Sudden Eclipse of Marigold Lambert

I had not been dead five minutes before Riley cupped his hand over Charity Sanborn's left breast, causing her to let out a silly giggle. I watched Riley, and that blond nurse he had hired to take care of me during my last days alive on this earth, carrying on like love-struck teenagers. I could see them while I lay unconscious in my own bed at home, and Charity Sanborn tucking my covers, adjusting the feeding tube in my stomach, the oxygen tubes in my nostrils, wiping streaks of bile from the edges of my mouth. All that while Riley stood at my deathbed, massaging her danger zones, working his hands up her rib cages and over her breasts, rubbing his groin into her backside.

I could see these visions in a way I cannot yet understand myself. I could see Charity Sanborn giggling and slapping at Riley. "Now, Mr. Riley. Please let me do my job." Her job was seducing Riley Lambert before his wife was dead, buried, and properly mourned. I know her type. That blond vulture.

In my dying, I watched them in living color, feeling myself busting loose from my body as a locust leaving its shell, as an egg separating white from yoke, a snake shedding skin. The part of me that separated from my body screamed at them, "I see you Riley Lambert. I see you Charity Sanborn. You miserable, indecent whores!"

I believe I was already dead before the doctor forced a tube down my windpipe and wired me to that machine that beeps like a false heart. I was floating outside myself already, watching, when a strange force gusted me around the hospital room. Untethered, I swirled across the nurses' white uniforms, melted into the lights, rolled under the bed, bumped softly against walls, floors, then to the ceiling, light as breath.

Outside myself, I watched Riley standing by the emergency room door, his hands in his pockets, shoulder against the doorframe.

"Is she dead?" Riley asked the doctor in the same voice that asks, "Is dinner ready?"

I floated against the ceiling above the doctor's balding head. With a jagged lurch I flashed back inside myself, felt the doctor's hands pressing against my face, the tube slipping inside my throat, my right hand death-gripping a nurse's arm. My left side felt as stiff and unbending as a dead tree. My blood felt like hot acid, an awful, hellish pain coursing through me. And then came the numbing cold, the left half of me frozen solid and the right half of me molten. Cold hell and hot hell, both.

"Marigold wouldn't want to be hooked up to those tubes. Unfasten her right now."

Riley's words gonged inside the church bell of my ears, and I put my hands to my metal head to stop the vibrating, and my fingers could not find the substance of my head, and then I went where the world is tipsy and I saw my hands drawn into clinched fists at the ends of my grey sweater sleeves.

The doctor explained to Riley that I would be on life support until he could determine the severity of my condition.

"I don't want Marigold hooked up if she's going to be a vegetable."

"That decision cannot be made yet," the doctor said.

Decision? I spiraled back along the twisted root of memory to my parents' sitting room.

Riley and I stood before my parents, the faces of several generations of dead relatives, aunts, uncles and grandparents, lined up on the mantle looking sternly from old black and white pictures, a long line of silent mouths set in fatal lines of resignation.

"You WILL marry Riley Lambert," Daddy said. "You WILL get married."

"I don't want to marry Riley," I said, seeing my daddy's eyes narrow, his mind snap shut.

In an instant, Daddy came off the settee to slap me. Mama came toward me sooner. She opened her mouth to say "NO," stepped in to catch Daddy's hand. Instead, she took the blow across her face. Blood came to the corner of her mouth. That motion picture has haunted me for thirty eight years. Now, I understand my mother, who had always kept the peace by passivity, had lived only in that one grand second when she had turned loose of her own self-consciousness, and acted from her heart.

My baby girl died at birth, soon after Riley and I were married. I remember the closed bud of her face, but I could not weep. In this dying, I felt closer kinship. I felt her waiting for me beyond the warp of time.

Riley stood at the hospital room door with his head down, frozen in his boots. He would have let my daddy slap me. He would let the doctor unhook my life. He would let Charity Sanborn make a fool of me in my own house.

I lived on in unconsciousness, but I did not live inside myself. I turned loose from my body. Floating above, I could view myself from any angle I chose, see my x-rayed bones moving in the fluid sac of my flesh. I could see through the architecture of the hospital, like the rooms of a doll's house. Eventually, I learned to *think* the irrational walls back to solid again. You cannot know this now, but in the beginning was the *thought*. Then came the *word*.

Hovering over my bed, I saw my body below me, plump, middle-aged, my chin fixed hard. My jowls hung slack. My eyelids floated half-opened. White tape fastened a tube that ran into my nose. An IV protruded from the large vein on the top of my hand. Wires ran from patches on my body to a monitor where my heart bleeped in thin blue lines. The nurses had taken off my garden shoes, my striped dress, and wrapped me in one of those hospital gowns that tie in the front.

When Riley brought my body home to escape the ruin of hospital bills, I followed. Riley turned the living room into a death room, this arrangement for convenience. All the bedrooms were upstairs.

Hired to care for me, Charity Sanborn came in starched white, carrying two suitcases. She took my husband Riley in the first sweep of her eyes, and then she took my home in the blinking. Charity had bleached hair worn neatly pinned under her nurses' cap. Her huge breasts pivoted like cannons on a battlefield. She wore an iron maiden bra with double cross supports. I judged her to be my age, fifty-five. I x-rayed the lines under her makeup. Mutton done up as lamb.

Riley brought her to my bedside. "My goodness. Marigold surely is too young to be in such a state." Charity set herself to work immediately checking my tubes, adjusting my pillow, studying the features of the comatose woman. She hovered above me. I hovered above her.

Charity Sanborn seemed too big for the room, one of those people who suck up all the air. Riley didn't take his eyes off her as she moved around my death bed in her scrubbed efficiency.

Charity brushed my hair. Oh, nurse-soldier that she was. My hair had gone grey. No more trips to the beauty parlor. Dying is not supposed to be beautiful, is it? Charity struggled the brush through the matted, tangled mess that she called deathbed hair.

Riley brought a pair of scissors and said, "Cut the tangles out."

"Now, Mr. Riley," Charity said. "I can untangle your wife's hair. See. I'll start here at the ends of her hair and work toward the roots."

After the brushing, Charity put my hair in a short braid and made iron grey spit curls upon my forehead. She powdered my face on either side of the oxygen tubes running into my nose. She painted my lips. She rouged my cheeks, making me up for the casket. Charity bade Riley approve of me with her false cheerfulness, with her petting of the blankets. He smiled his little crooked smile while I viewed my grotesque reflection in his eyes.

Charity's everlasting goodwill and patience stamped itself upon Riley. He hated seeing me withering away in my deathbed, but loved how Charity cared that I was dying. I floated upon the wall behind my bed. I watched Charity adjust the morphine pump, change my soiled diaper. I studied her false smile, the way her eyes circled back to see if Riley was watching her, and I understood that she was conscious of her own deceit.

"The least we can do is make Marigold comfortable during her final days," said Charity. I hated her calling me Marigold. I hated her reducing my authority to that of a child's.

My final days? I saw lights during my final days. Flashes of light. Polka dotted lights. Tornadoes of light. The lights were coming for me. I wanted to turn completely loose and go. I could not think myself loose from life. When I could not think myself loose from Riley, I heard thunder. I saw lightning strike the room. I watched a storm move across the bed.

"Will she hang on much longer?" Riley said. "I mean will Marigold have to suffer this way much longer? Like a vegetable?"

"You can never really tell, Mr. Riley," Charity said.

She called my husband Mr. Riley. Oh, she knew every ingratiating trick. Mr. Riley?

Respectful, but personal.

"I'll know the signs, Mr. Riley. Short of that we must be patient."

Charity Sanborn needed me alive. She needed time to make Riley dependent upon her. I understood Charity Sanborn's motives as well as she did.

You must separate yourself from your own body in order to understand things clearly. But you cannot know that now. What if I tell you that you will stay married for thirty eight years to a man because you do not know how to leave? You think that he will change. He never does. He thinks that you will always stay the same. You never can. Meanwhile, you live in the illusion of habit. Eating Cheerios for breakfast, watching re-runs of the Andy Griffith Show, packing his favorite peanut butter and dill pickle sandwiches in his lunch box, getting your flu shots each fall, paying the electric bill, buying groceries, voting, reading the newspapers, making pot roast for Sunday dinner.

Living is a comfortable illusion. The things of your heart that scream out to be heard are pressed down and packed away inside you like old linens. Time passes at the bottom of the drawer. Time stands still in the rush of daily routine. Then, you are on your knees in the dirt, gouging out the stubborn roots of a cow vine that has smothered the begonias, wondering if the meat loaf in the oven should be attended, and suddenly, the sun goes into eclipse, and the life you thought you never really wanted ends in the flower bed.

You would be surprised to know that many other women besides Charity Sanborn wanted Riley, too. Well-meaning widows from the church came with coconut cake and beef Stroganoff, bearing their special recipes before them like sacrificial gifts to the altar. But Charity had staked the territory of Riley's heart for herself. She never allowed these women to cross the threshold. If they stood tip-toe to peek inside the house, Charity squared her shoulders and leaned forward like a Mac Truck. "Mr. Lambert isn't home," she'd say, even if Riley was upstairs reading the newspaper. "Mr. Lambert doesn't want visitors. Marigold is in a coma. This ordeal is difficult enough for him."

Charity made their coming seem inconsiderate. She closed the door abruptly leaving them standing with their soufflé dishes in hand. Charity understood they'd have to return to pick up their bowl, therefore, they should not be allowed to enter. Two birds. One stone.

Did I say that Charity Sanborn rearranged my furniture to suit her own taste?

"You know, Mr. Riley, that sideboard would really look better against that wall," she'd say.

In a flash, Riley had the house turned completely around. Charity made sure he'd switched his bedroom furniture to the spare room on the opposite end of the house. A new room. A new woman. No flashbacks from a previous bedroom allowed.

Did I tell you that Charity Sanborn sold my heirlooms to an antiques dealer, to a Mrs. Biddle, a short, stocky woman, a friend of Charity's? She came wearing a shabby raincoat and carrying an absurd umbrella with ducks quacking around the edge. She bought my doll collection for a fraction of its value. She paid a song for my trundle bed, for my great-grandmother's butter churn, the wooden dough bowl, for all my family treasures. Riley called these pieces of my heritage the junk of the past. Charity agreed the house would look less cluttered. I had no need for these things, now, she said. I needed Riley to want to cling to something that I cherished. Maybe I could love him then, even if that meant vegetable love.

When Charity and Riley first knew the heat of their luxurious passion, I learned to blow cold. Riley first came to her bedroom after she had conveniently bumped into him in the dark hallway, her timing always perfect. She wore a see-through negligee.

While they wallowed in the upstairs hallway, I thought myself into an icy blast. I traveled up Charity's spine and down the crevices of her huge bosom.

Charity Sanborn screamed and shivered. Riley must have thought she screamed for him until I rushed inside his mouth and blew at the back of his throat and came out his nose as frozen fog. And then I traveled to regions below and froze an icicle there. Charity bounced him off, screaming.

"It's Marigold." she said. "She's here."

Charity took Riley under the warmth of her covers and explained death to him. She had cared for the dying many times. A doppelganger, she called me. He seemed uncomfortable with the idea that I might be loosed from my body, watching him after all, like God invisible.

"Don't worry," she told him, "Don't be afraid of the cold."

Charity took me on, a contest of wills. She openly courted Riley, brought his hands to her private places, even at my deathbed, and smiled at the empty room.

Perhaps you think that in the topsy-turvy space of death there is forgiveness. You cannot know this now, but in your dying state all of your suppressed anger will rise green and ugly like a dead frog to the top of the cistern. You will look upon the waters and see your own ugly face. But this viewing is not like looking into a mirror. Your mirror image is but a pantomime of yourself, every movement a synchronized counter movement in the looking glass. In death, you will observe yourself in the same way you observe the grocer bagging your food, in the same way you observe the woman while she is stealing your husband. While she is suctioning the bile from your throat and your husband comes up behind her and he is thrusting his hands up the back of her white uniform to find her place of heat. While she is standing at your bed, unbuttoning her uniform, smiling down on you because she knows that you know. While your husband is having his way with the woman who is charged with keeping you alive, you die a different death. The death of the body is a simple matter compared to the death of the spirit. Or had you not thought the spirit dies, too?

I wanted to harm Charity. I wanted to gouge her eyes, yank out her hair, bite off her ears, stick the syringe into her brain. But in the end, my pathetic assaults were simply cold air, an inconvenience at the back of her neck.

I expected Charity to dilute the sludge-food that gurgled through the feeding tube into my stomach, suppress the oxygen, or pump the morphine too many times. Charity, however, was tediously patient and careful. Her uprightness impressed Riley all the more. Meanwhile, the days waxed and waned, the seasons of planting and growing passed. In early fall, I died the second and final time when the sign was in the heart, when that which has been uprooted can never grow back again.

Charity called Riley into the death room one evening. "Our Marigold is leaving us." She wiped at false tears. "You won't be needing me much longer, Mr. Riley."

I had now shrunken to the size of a child, my body curled into the fetal position, blood settled into my eye sockets and turned dark, my mouth gaped wide open, my lips stretched across my teeth, the final howl on my face.

You might think that letting go is easy. You are wrong. Letting go is impossible. You will stitch the last thread of your willpower to the people in the very room you hate, to the lives of the very people you hate. You will cling to Charity Sanborn's packed suitcases, to the sound of her heels on the pavement and the slammed door, to the sound of Riley Lambert shaking out the Sunday newspaper where the obituary and picture appear, the one where you and Riley are square dancing at the senior center.

"Let go of that memory," you say. "Let go."

No use. No use. The umbilical cord of hate stretches so impossibly thin you are sure it will snap, and yet, you warp and spin farther, and father still, not ever breaking free.

Marlene L'Abbé
The Unveiling

Catherine Carter

A long story

It's a long story, you say to me, a stranger
trying to read on a bus. No,
I think, it's not, or it needn't be,
as my thumbs itch to snatch
your neck like a dog with a chuck—
a big dog, her wrath sung in a rare, deep bay—
and shake, shake. Or maybe it's the personal
pronouns that make it grate,
all the things you sensed,
how complicated you are.
Or maybe it's the lack of pauses.
Ten thousand years is a long story,
mostly pauses: the shift and slide of empires
and rock faces, the passage of law. *Let me explain*,
you say ominously, and then,
do you know what I'm saying? as if
there were any hope of not knowing
what you're saying. Summarize,
I think, with marrow-
deep rage. Try a topic sentence.
Toss me the chop bone
of a spotted 400-pound sow
whose story was as complicated as yours,
her sufferings as deep, or the wristbone
of the woman on yesterday's bus.
Her neighbor asked something blessedly
inaudible. She answered—her daughter
had died—and stopped,
glanced through the pane
of smeared glass at the gray river.
That, I think, that is a long story,
that story will go on forever.

Catherine Carter

Devil's walking stick
—for M.C.

You grasp it first by accident,
maybe, when you've lost your way
in the woods and are skidding down
a muddy bank, lash out a hand to brace
yourself straight into the electric
exploding thrill of perforation, chime
of adrenaline as the toxic spines slide
into your palm like they've always
belonged there, like they evolved a million
years for this and so did your hand
for this moment, this meeting.
All through recovery's seethe and swell
you remember too that sickening
sparkle of venom, the way it wiped out
all your fear of the bonebreak fall,
all that bellystone worry whether
you'd ever get home or survive
finding it again if you did. The devil's
walking-stick's inner bark is good
for toothache; turns out it's good
for other pains too, so soon enough
comes moment you're staring up
at that thorny shaft crowned with rough
froths of bloom white as cocaine,
and you touch a finger to the tiniest
tingling hair, its carillon along your nerves
liquor-gold and as rich in oblivion,
a deadening splinter working in,
and by fall you're back in those scrubby
second-growth woods every day,
one spine or three not enough
anymore, beginning to suck the fruits'
purple-black drupes, though they make
you sick, as you knew they would.
And late that year you finally cut
yourself a staff of the devil's holey
wood, long enough to draw a circle
of protection between you and everything

else, a wall of thorns no anguish can cross
as long as you grasp that nettle.
People keeping asking why
are you doing this, why don't you stop,
why can't you just put it down?
And part of you wants to, part
of you wants them to lock you up
and make you stop, but it would be easier
to just stop puking mid-heave,
just stop the berries' burning diarrhea
when the cramps torque down:
you need to clutch these quivering quills,
press your hand to those spurs
until they prick clear to the heart
and let it stutter to rest, you are
the only devil here now
and this barbellate stick is what it takes
to let you keep hobbling along,
envenomed, inside your piercing life.

Catherine Carter

Song for a housekeeper

—for Bonnie, Ellen, Rita, Toby, Lorraine, Alex, Griffin, and Penny Jo

Her dustbin's soft with human hair
and dark with grit of displaced earth,
enough shed skin to make a man.
The plate from which she wipes black marks,
like fingerprints from the doorframe,
constrains pent lightning in the wall
in unseen runnels of blue flame.
Her upraised hand draws water forth,
invoked into the plastic pail's
black chalice to dissolve despair
and scour a hallway clean as rain.
She starts in the north on each floor,
and draws the circle with her feet,
works out from the elevator,
spindle on which the building turns.
Few know the strength in her right arm,
cocked back to chivy entropy
with the wide mop; few recognize
her vacuum summoning cyclones,
tying their whirl into a sack,
commanding, with her steady craft,
the poles of atoms to align
to make the cosmos orderly,
as her god calls her by her name,
which relatively few here know,
though we'd do well to do the same.

Valerie Nieman

My Own

The loader at Home Depot
asks who is putting this together
for me
and I answer,
      I am,

and I do,
because I am become
my own husband,
having been poorly husbanded—
no, let's be real, shepherded.
Left shorn, nicked, bloodied, and bleating
with outrage.

I am my own father,
using his tools (a few)
and those he bought me
(after #2)
liveried in yellow and black,
tools no better than mediocre,
an undersized hammer
and wonky wrench.

I am my own brother, too,
at times pulling on
the guise of absent son,
the one who stayed
only long enough
to leave a laceration.

I am
my own
here in the dark;
here in the dark
I am.

Valerie Nieman

Don't Be an Old Woman
—after Sara Teasdale

After it rains, then I can go outside.
(peek through the slats)

If it rains then the hell-heart
afternoon will relent

and I can walk without hazard.
(code red — don't be a fool)

Rain comes now like thunder
even when there is no thunder,

driven by heat, pelting hail-hard
on lashing winds, smashing the garden.

There will come no more soft
rains breeding red efts and fireflies

out of the belabored land.
(we've brewed our cup of poison)

Let the water come down,
let that heat fade to chill,

sink to my spine,
become familiar.

Valerie Nieman

Men Talk at the Griffith Garage

You gotta start it just so
give it the gas but light
don't pump it.

Carburetor wants
about this much gas
this much air.

Too lean it stutters
give it too much
it'll flood out.

A bit tetchy.
Gotta let that old big
block V8 warm up.

She wants to run.

Deni Naffziger

A Tale of Two Women

Today I make gazpacho while Joe is dying.
My husband picks tomatoes and cucumbers,

carries them to the kitchen like he always does.
I peel Oxhearts. Billie holds her husband's hand,

traces the soft spaces between his tendons,
circles the bone of his wrist,

while I slice vegetables into quarters,
then eighths, then turn them

from vertical to horizontal.
She empties the urinal, and I scoop seeds

from the cutting board,
wipe it dry.

An entire jalapeño seems too much,
so I halve it.

Another dose of morphine,
he closes his eyes.

Wendy McVicker

Hope is the thing with butter

On the darkest day
of a dark year, I gather
these simple ingredients—

butter, flour, sugar—
fold them together
with a wooden spoon

the way your grandmother
did, then roll the dough
thin—round disc

of December sun low
on the horizon.

Score with rays, sprinkle
rosemary for remembrance—
oh, we remember—

and bake to golden goodness.
Swallowing those fragrant
triangles, we savor hope,

warm our throats
as the earth turns
once again to the light

and we turn with her

Diana Ferguson
Life is Magical

Elaine Fowler Palencia

The Sandwich Wizard

You doing all right today? What'll it be? Whoa, slow down. This is the first sandwich of the rest of your life. Don't be too previous. What kind of bread? I've got white, whole wheat, and sourdough.

White it is. Mustard? Yellow or Dijon?

All right: Dijon. I like to repeat everything. Nothing worse than a misunderstood sandwich. Years ago, there was a boy worked here named Dijon. Talk about spicy. Mayonnaise? Gotta be careful here. You have to handle fresh bread with kitty gloves so it don't tear. See, I use this little spatula to feather the dressings. Use a lot of delicate wrist action.

I nearly had a holiday today. When I woke up, it was snowing cross-legged and cold as a pawnbroker's heart in January. After I got myself all shoveled out, come to find out my doors was froze shut. And here I am going through the Change, uphill both ways. If I could channel them hot flashes, I'd a-melted them doors free. I called in and Don said, get your husband to bring you. I said, you've not been paying attention if you think I've got a husband laying around. Old Don had to come and get me and Charlene, which her truck wouldn't start. He can't drive for shit. We're lucky to be above ground.

You people form a line. I'll be with you in two shakes of a lamb's tail.

Now then. At this point I lay down a leaf of lettuce, which you didn't say you wanted lettuce but it's important for the color contrast. We all need contrast. Ham, roast beef, turkey, or tuna? Smoked or Italian herb? Turkey reminds me of Cousin Ruth, pore old soul, had a neck like a turkey gobbler. That kindly turned me off turkey myself. You get three slices. I fold each one like turning down covers on a bed, and then fold the next one down and the next, and stack 'em staggered. Pretty as a baby's butt. That artist Pistachio couldn't do better.

Tomato? A woman come in here the other day and said they're raising square tomatoes—easier to ship. I used to work with her in Morehead; know her same as the paint on the wall. Cheese? I wouldn't worry about cholesterol. If you drink two tablespoons of cider vinegar after you eat, it won't stick to your arteries. I got American, Swiss, cheddar, Munster and mozzarella. My boy loved to watch the Munsters on TV. They don't have many channels where he is now, but I've got a little set on layaway for when he gets out next month. It was the drinking done him in. He could get drunk in a salad bar.

If you don't mind my saying, that mozzarella's going to be awful bland with the turkey. I'd kick it up a notch to Swiss. Cheddar'll overwhelm it. And how about a pickle on the side? It'll run you extra, but the way I see it, a sandwich without a pickle is like a car without a hood ornament. I know, there's a lot of that going around. Sold! You won't regret it.

There you are, all spick and spandy. Toasted? Do you want it cut in two rectangles or two triangles? Some people like to nibble the points. I knew a man divorced his wife for cutting his sandwiches down the middle instead of corner to corner. Well, that and a few other things. He could turn mean as a striped snake.

Chips? What kind? Take your time. And about my boy, it'd been different if his daddy had stuck around, or if Mama hadn't been the way she was, or say we could've afforded to live in a nicer section or if I had went to school longer and maybe learned parenting. It's a thing they actually teach now. His daddy and me, we were ideally unsuited.

Receipt? Cross my palm with money and I'll tell your fortune.

Still and all, it's not for sure he'll get out next month, but we don't talk about that when I visit. I just tell him, try to see every day like a sandwich. First, choose your daily bread and lay the two slices out like an open book. Then, pick what you want to put in the book. It's YOUR book. Take as much time as you need for it to all fit together. Keep doing that day after day, concentrating on them choices. Like Mama said, don't worry about the mule going blind; just load the wagon.

You bet. You have a good one, too.

Morning. You doing all right today? What'll it be?

Lisa Kwong

8th Grader at the Mercy of a Bus Pan

Every Sunday lunch rush, Daddy moves
like an octopus doing kung fu
when he's stir-frying and shouting
orders at Mommy and Uncle,
and the waiters hoist up
trays on their hands, wrists
perfectly bent to balance
heavy plates. I help host,
but it's so busy I have to start
bussing tables to keep up:
parties of 10,15, even 20,
without reservations, crowd
the entrance, fill every bar stool.
I grab half-full water cups, plates
stained with sweet and sour chicken,
half-eaten lo mein, and cheeseburgers;
wipe up salt and sugar piles on plexiglass.
Then, CRASH! Glass, ceramic, silverware!
Jumping, I throw my rag, watch it rise, fall.

The restaurant goes silent. Customers stare.
It's a wonder everything didn't fall out
or break. I've made a mess of this unbalanced
bus pan! Chaotic chorus resumes; in some corners,
I hear soft laughter, imagine they pity my clumsiness.
I work faster to clear the floor, grimacing, because
they don't know what it's like to work weekends
while my friends giggle and gossip at sleepovers,
don't have to worry about demanding, sometimes angry,
customers who don't care that I'm just a kid. They don't
know about going home with tiny cracks all over my hands
from cleaning up other people's messes all day. I wish
they would tell me it's okay rather than chuckle
at my fallen bus pan. It's easy to laugh
when you're sitting comfortable, crunching your egg rolls
and chicken chow mein with family, oblivious to waiters
whirling by with steaming hot tea and fried noodles,
oblivious to the humiliation of a girl who wants
to spend Sunday playing with her younger siblings
or singing along to Mariah Carey on her boombox.

Lisa Kwong

Searching for Wonton Soup

Nothing compares to Mom and Dad's wontons, mini globes
of ground pork perfectly wrapped in a thin golden skin. But
I can't live at home forever just to be fed. At every restaurant
in Bloomington, Indiana, I try to find a soup good enough:

broth not too oily, skin tender as the meat inside. I love
dozens of crisp scallions floating like emeralds, slick green
baby bok choy steamed just enough. I've been satisfied,
disappointed. Sometimes I wonder what the hell I just ate.

I hate going out to eat with complainers, even though we all can cook
better than what we pay for. Sometimes we don't want to dice
vegetables, or we tire of flipping and stabbing meat with silver
thermometers. We just want to eat. Once in China, my father saw his mother

staring into a soup kitchen window crowded with customers scooping up
wontons and slurping broth, as steam rose to cloud the ceiling. She clasped
her hands behind her back, her face full of hunger. Seamstress money
wasn't enough to buy bowls full of wontons for herself, her husband,

and six children. Dad tells me I don't know struggle, not like they knew
in Tai Shan or when his feet first touched ground in San Francisco,
when English was a diamond locked in a glass case. I will never
fully understand their poverty: imprints on shoulders and hands
from carrying buckets of water from a well, cooking rice over open fire,

living in a one room brick house with dirt floor, sleeping in heat
while mosquitoes siphoned their sweet blood. Now filled with gratitude,
I know there are worse things than bad wonton soup. Because they had little,
my father now prepares enough for an army in training: plates overflowing
with beef, yu choy, chicken, broccoli, and shrimp on every table.
We fear hunger, fear necessities running out, so we buy extra, cook extra,
wonder: when will anything ever be enough?

Neema Avashia

Appalachian *Asimina*

My first thought upon seeing the handful of paw paws my father brought home one day in the early 1980s: This fruit is ugly. Maybe the ugliest of native West Virginia fruits I'd encountered so far. It possessed neither the mystical translucence of the gooseberry, nor the gleaming, jeweled exterior of a wineberry. Instead, it looked like some strange mix of potato and papaya, greenish-brown with black spots. When dad sliced it open, he revealed a creamy yellow interior, pocked with large brown seeds. The grainy flesh possessed a sweet and mild flavor that fell somewhere between that of a banana and a mango.

My second thought: So *this* is what we've been singing about in Mrs. Moore's music class, where my English-language-learner self parroted lines without understanding what they meant. "Pickin' up paw paws, put 'em in a basket. Pickin' up paw paws, put 'em in a basket. Pickin' up paw paws, put 'em in a basket. Way down yonder in the paw paw patch."

The paw paw is the only American member of the *Asimina* family, a custard apple pushed from the tropics into my mountain home by wooly mammoths and ground sloths 18,000 years ago. The Appalachian cousin of the sitafal that my father loved to eat growing up in India, and the guanabana that my Dominican middle school students love to put in their batidos. The mountain banana, as some folks call it, begins as a dark purple blossom on trees each spring across Appalachia, and ripens in mid-September, but you won't find it in most chain grocery stores. Only in local markets, or family farms, or growing wild in the woods, or sold out of a truck on the side of a winding one-lane road.

There was much my Indian family didn't understand about Appalachia when we moved there in the late 70s, from accents to music to foodways. Much we had to figure out in our attempts to find home in a community where our Brown skin, our Gujarati, our Hinduism set us on the outside from the outset. Survival in the context of such isolation demanded that we learn to code-switch, and learn quickly. And we found many willing teachers: My dad's boss, Dr. Sexton, taught us the rules of Appalachian gardening. My adopted grandmother, Mrs. Bupp, taught us the rules of Appalachian food. Mr. Starcher, who lived down the street, taught us the rules of Appalachian neighboring. Each lesson, each interaction, unlocking another kernel of belonging. Knowledge of the paw paw brought me closer to my classmates, closer to the community where I was born. A glimmer of insider status that showed me membership might indeed be possible. And when I got a mid-September Fedex box of paw paws and gooseberries sent to me overnight a few years ago, straight from the hills of Kenna to the streets of Jamaica Plain, it reminded me that though I may have quit West Virginia in moving to Boston, West Virginia has not, as yet, quit me.

Most fruits taken out of their tropical context would die in the deciduous biome. After all, have you ever seen a mango tree in the mountains? Custard apples in the tropics are fragile and tender, easily opened by bare hands when ripe. Still the paw paw survived in the new world. It thickened its skin to ward off bad weather, widened its leaves to absorb more sunlight, just as we thickened our skins to ward off racial slurs, and widened our friend circle to include not just Indian aunties and uncles, but also White West Virginians.

But when work disappeared, my family left West Virginia, scattered to the Northeast and the Southwest in search of better economic climes much the way my parents had when leaving India, much the way the wooly mammoth and the ground sloth had when they made their journey northwards during the Ice Age. Leaving was not optional. Leaving was survival.

A fellow displaced West Virginian who lives an hour from me sprouted a paw paw tree from seed a few years ago, planted it in the ground in his New England backyard. Each spring we wait to see if it will flower and bear fruit. If the paw paw can find a way to evolve once again.

Jessica Cory

Farmer's Market: A Ghazal

Every Saturday in the county's DMV parking lot, folks gather.
Farmers selling corn, strawberries, crops they've gathered

from soil they've planted and hoed, watered and talked to,
or at least talked about, with friends and family who gather

together at the feed store, or the guitar shop, or the kitchen
table. They rinse the lettuce and tomatoes and eggs gathered

shortly after dawn, when the chicken shit is still caked on
and dew beads ripple off leaves in rivulets, a puddle gathering

the drops before the Earth quenches its thirst. A sign
swings from the white pop-up tent above a gathering

of three-berry jam, flowers, and rhubarb: *Cory Farms,*
Oldest Family Farm in Ross County. My ancestors still gather.

Jessica Cory

The Land After Time: A Sestina

Dinosaurs. My five-year-
old son is obsessed with them & the periods
in which they lived, learning the plants,
cycads that grew before trees.
We've watched *The Land Before Time*
more times than I can count.

I cannot count
the number of years,
cannot track the number of times
I've read the words between each period
that spoke of which animals, which trees
were extinct. Those memories implanted

like roots within my brain. I plant
tomatoes each Spring, counting
on them to grow, that the tulip tree
gracing our front yard will stand another year.
Yet each year the wet & dry periods
make it clear that we're running out of time.

How much longer until it's time
we realize that the exploitation we've planted
comes home to roost? What happens when our period
is over? Yes, will be become extinct. We can count
on that fact. Maybe not this year or next year,
but I've seen *Life After People* & the trees

will grow rich in our absence. Maple & live oak trees
will gather rings as I have firewood, marking their time,
lining the cambium year after year after glorious year
undoing the damage humanity wrought, replanting
themselves, too many to count, but there is no one to count
them anyway. There may be periods of ice, periods

of fire, periods of drought & rain, but like all periods
they end; they are portals to what comes next. Trees
will grow & die & fall & evolve; this can be counted
on. But what is counting but a form of time?

Human time is futile, we will be supplanted,
maybe even by new dinosaurs, in the coming years.

I cannot count the periods I've had over the years,
but may the tree roots use my blood to mend the soil, to plant
new beginnings, countless possibilities in their remaining time.

Kristine Williams

At the Preschool, Lunch

You think *I just can't*
because creativity got lost at some point
between chasing James
as he looks over his shoulder and heads right for the mud puddle
at top four-year-old speed
which is faster than you imagine
and slightly faster than you can catch up
mud that Maria Montessori said children should explore
but that parents seem to see as a personal affront
and do you know how much those shoes cost and
he only has the one pair since his feet grow so quickly
between that
and telling Ruby that no
the binky stays in the cubby
because she bit her friend
and her mother decided that this would be a good time to
break the habit she apparently relied on
for four years and wants teachers
paid less than Ohio's minimum wage
but more than other preschools
at least that's what the director reiterates
you swear
every single day
breaking the binky habit now enforced at school
although you saw them at Kroger this weekend
and there
in the cereal aisle
mom plugged that sucker into a screaming
i-want-i-want mouth
and you walked by without a word
but deliberately
convinced that the parents hate you
and send salmon for the smell
when reheated in the microwave
for a toddler
mind you
or the rice and the noodles
sticking to the floor as you try to use the broom
under and around tiny chairs

make order of food chaos
try
at least
then
nap time and the puzzle of Libby needs quiet
and Jasper needs to be away from the toys and
right in the middle of losing your mind
the most challenging of the toddlers
the one who scares you just a little
because she knows exactly which buttons to
not push
but slam
and who sucks every bit of patience
and intellect out through your ears
and just when you are ready to snap
that little red head
throws her pudgy arms around your neck unexpectedly
and hugs the stuffing out of you
and you find some balance again and
sit on the floor between two cots
rub circles on tiny backs
and thank whatever god is there
for finding what moves you
most days to tears.

Kristine Williams

In The Dark

At an hour no one should see alone,
my husband's snores vibrate in my chest

when I pad, barefoot,
tip toe through the bedroom for fuzzy socks,

echoes in the wood of this house
we share, have shared,

enough years
to raise two children,

pack trucks we rented with teen detritus—
lift, carry, drive, unload, drive away.

Later, we write checks for others
to pack trucks with more of their collected stuff,

one flies to the east coast,
one now to the west.

II.

Bare patches on the hillside
have filled with crocus,

scattered by the handful years ago,
A riot of purples, some yellow, overspill

the furrows where they pulled the trash truck out,
the one that slid backward down an icy hill,

nearly into the pond,
where the sudden cold stunned peepers into silence.

Weeks later they came, pulled the truck out with a winch,
offered free trash service for life.

III.

I once planted a burning bush,
watched the twig I ordered from a local company

that specialized in deer resistant
(as if there is such a thing) foliage,

grow wildly out of control.
I cut it down last year, shaggy and blocking the driveway,

the suckers, tiny reaching fingers,
ghosts of brilliant red

that flared, then
littered the ground after the first cold rain.

Michele Binegar
Wilderness of Patience

Carter Taylor Seaton

May I have your autograph?

It arrived, inauspiciously, in a small, ivory, vellum envelope, much like the RSVP insert for a wedding invitation. The engraved return address on the back read, *"Ladies' Home Journal,"* followed by the magazine's address in New York City. Assuming it was an advertising solicitation, albeit an expensive one, for our small craft organization, Appalachian Craftsmen, Inc. to put an ad in this prestigious women's magazine, I nevertheless opened it.

"Dear Ms. Seaton," it read, "you have been nominated for the Ladies' Home Journal Women of the Year 1975 Award." It went on to state the date of the awards presentation at a New York theatre and included an invitation from the magazine's publisher, Lenore Hershey, to dine with her at Rockefeller Center before the event. Clearly, this was no solicitation, and just as clearly it was a mistake. Me? Woman of the Year? Me, director of a rural craft cooperative in West Virginia? How on earth did the *Ladies' Home Journal* even know I existed?

After many moments of shock, I re-read the letter, which explained the annual awards presented by the magazine and saw the response card. Now I realized fully that it was not a joke, nor a solicitation. Each year, *Ladies Home Journal* honored women for achievement in various fields such as entertainment, politics, government, education, communication, the arts— both visual and literary—and community service. It was the latter category in which I'd been nominated for directing Appalachian Craftsmen, Inc., a rural, craft cooperative that gave women an opportunity to supplement their families' income through the home production of patchwork and quilted clothing, home decorator items, and toys. Initially, the organization had been co-sponsored by a community action agency and the Junior League of Huntington, West Virginia. In its formative years, I'd been a Junior League volunteer helping to shape the bylaws, the mission statement, and the organization's operational manual. Once it was ready to launch, the board tapped me to be its executive director.

Now, four years later the invitation was like being told I had been granted fairy princess status, including a weekend in New York with the possibility of a national award—all broadcast live on television. For a thirty-something woman with a house to keep clean, laundry to do, four kids, dogs, cats, a duck, and a horse this would be an alternative reality. Cincinnati was *my* big city. Suddenly, I'd been invited to New York City.

For my husband, his pride in me made the decision a no-brainer. Of course, we would go. Since the Junior League held a suite of rooms at the Waldorf Astoria that members could reserve for $40 a night, we quickly made reservations, and booked our flight on Allegheny Airlines. A weekend in the Big Apple. What could be better? I was feeling pretty special by then. Oh God, what could I wear? On our limited budget, a dress fancy enough to wear to dinner at Rockefeller Center or this ceremony certainly didn't live in my closet. A floor-length red cotton dress with a sleeveless shirred top would have to do. Besides, it looked dressy when I added faux pearls.

New York sparkled in the August sunlight as we landed. Outside La Guardia, yellow cabs lined the sidewalk. We took the first one that didn't have his OUT OF SERVICE sign lighted. Despite the distance to Manhattan, we should have walked. The cab smelled like a cheaply-perfumed lady of the night and that she and her greasy-haired john had been his last fare. The driver spoke limited English and drove like a stereotypical New York cabbie. He cut in and out of traffic at breakneck speed, narrowly missed two men crossing the street, and screamed "sombitch" at everyone in his way. We gripped the back of the seat in front of us until I thought I'd tear the worn fabric. When we encountered a traffic jam, he simply drove the wrong way on a one-way street. He was the one the other drivers should have been calling "sombitch." It wasn't an auspicious beginning to the fairy tale.

We arrived at the doors of the Waldorf in a sweat, glad for our lives, and trying desperately to regain the composure we believed befitting the hotel. While the hotel's swanky lobby, with its storied clock tower and thick carpets, didn't disappoint, the room was not as large as our bedroom at home. That's what you get for $40 in New York, I thought.

The ceremony, which was to be televised live by CBS, was set for Saturday night. If we were in New York, we were going to do it up right. Theater ticket prices were $7 for the cheap seats and $15 for good seats, so we decided to splurge. We may never get this chance again. Between arrival on Friday afternoon, we squeezed in a Friday night play, a Saturday matinee, and a Sunday matinee. On Friday night as we watched Richard Kiley reprise his original role in a revival of *The Man of la Mancha*, we spotted the theater critic Gene Shalit in the audience.

During intermission, while my husband was in the restroom, Mr. Shalit approached me and put out his hand. "Hello, Carter," he said, as if we'd known each other for years. "It's good to see you. Will you be at the dinner tomorrow night? If so, I'll see you there." Flummoxed, I stammered that I would. How in the world did he know me? He couldn't have, of course. My husband returned to our seats with a shit-eating grin on his face, and I knew. He'd asked the famous man to say hello.

Award night arrived. We safely cabbed it to Rockefeller Center where Lenore Hershey, the magazine's gracious editor, and a member of her staff met us in the lobby. Suddenly, I felt as if I were in a dream as our elevator sped toward the top floor of the skyscraper. When we alighted, the floor looked like an ordinary office building, closed doors lining the hall. Then we turned and entered a large suite set with a long well-appointed dining table. Places were marked with engraved place-cards. Not knowing a single soul, except our new acquaintance, Ms. Hershey, we awkwardly began looking for our seats. We took them and soon the table began to fill. As we met our fellow diners, it became clear most worked for the magazine, until Alan Alda and his wife, along with two of their three daughters, entered the room and took their seats. Everyone's favorite actor! And I was having dinner with him! I couldn't believe it. Wait until I tell Mother; she loves M.A.S.H., I thought. Throughout dinner I tried to think of something witty to say to him, if I got the chance. But, he talked as fast as he ate, mostly about his girls, who stared into their plates, looking as embarrassed as my kids would have, had I done the same in public.

By eight o'clock the tiny theater was nearly full. Not nearly as large as the ones we'd been in Friday or that afternoon, this one was set up for broadcasting what was on stage. It might have been used for *The Price is Right* or another game show, so the audience was up close and often a part of the show. Just before the doors closed, a group of teenage school girls rushed in. It appeared the show's producers wanted a full and hearty audience, even if they hadn't been invited, so they had admitted these girls.

The house lights dimmed, but not until after I'd read the program and learned that I wouldn't be walking on stage to receive an award. A woman from Texas who had organized a half-way home for female ex-prisoners did. I had thought the awards would come as a surprise announcement, but I soon realized the magazine would have had to tell all the nominees to be sure they attended. This avoided awkward pauses if they announced a winner's name and they weren't in the audience.

I recovered, and actually breathed a sigh of relief. I hadn't realized I was nervous at the thought of crossing that stage. Now, I relaxed and watched women whose names I'd only read in the news, watched on television, or in the movies cross that stage. The great Barbara Jordan, the first black congresswoman from the Deep South spoke after receiving her award. Her sonorous voice and deep accent vibrated the air. Marlo Thomas, her black hair in a perfect flip crossed the stage in three-inch heels and a mini-skirt that revealed her long, slender legs. Florence Henderson bubbled in her role as Mistress of Ceremonies. Each woman had a story that revealed fully the rightness of their award. I couldn't have held a candle to them, not even the Texas winner in my category. Still, by being nominated, my work to help low-income women supplement their family incomes had been recognized. While I'd never expected accolades for what I was doing, I did feel it was important and rewarding work, but having it acknowledged nationally gave me a great sense of accomplishment. And, I'd been treated to a magical weekend. Who could have a single regret on such a night?

As the curtain came down, I made my way to the stage to thank Mrs. Hershey. The audience was leaving, the curtain had been raised to break down the sets, and several of the famous winners were on stage including Marlo Thomas and Florence Henderson. As I talked with Mrs. Hershey, I could hear that several of the young girls who had arrived late were also on the stage seeking autographs from the actresses. As I turned to leave, they approached me as well. One girl asked, "May we have your autograph? Please?"

I hesitated briefly, then took the pad and pen. "Certainly," I said as I wrote. "My best, Carter Seaton." They squealed and went to look for others to add to their collection. I walked back up the aisle toward my husband with a huge smile on my face. In the future, as they show that autograph book to their daughters, they're going to wonder, "who the hell was Carter Seaton." I had given my first and only autograph. But, it was enough.

The fairy tale ended. Life with four kids, a house, and laundry awaited me. But, as they say, I'll always have New York, and that autograph seeker.

Jayne Moore Waldrop

Bird Bones

The bright, slick watercraft arrived with blaring Bluetooth speakers, a full range of speed and sound, an investment in their next chapter. They had survived careers, childrearing, his prostate cancer treatment, her osteoporosis diagnosis. They figured they had earned this fiberglass symbol of freedom.

Before taking the Jet Ski for a test run, he adjusted his glasses and read the instruction manual cover to cover, concentrating on the fine print, absorbing how to safely operate the wasplike vehicle across the lake's broad expanse. Grimacing as he read, he learned of hazards he'd never before connected to having fun—a serious risk of head, anal or vaginal injuries from falling off backwards.

"It'll rip you a new one," he warned her, then he ordered neoprene shorts for them both. It wasn't their best look.

They launched, going easy at first, taking turns at the helm, milking the throttle white-knuckled as they passed a towboat pushing a long line of barges. They grew more adventurous with each trip then hit their stride at speeds they'd have forbidden their youthful kin. Daily they covered fresh territory, found unexplored bays filled with waterlilies and birds that glistened like beautiful flying machines as the humans and aves moved in tandem near the surface. They witnessed eagles, osprey, Canadas, egrets, and great blue herons, sometimes holding poses undisturbed or treading calmly, sometimes lifting off, their massive wings stroking the sky to find a rising air current to ride.

One glorious day with brilliant blue skies dotted by cotton-ball clouds, they decided to head to the bird sanctuary across the lake. Most days they shared a feeling of not wanting to miss out on anything, even when she felt dog-tired, almost droopy, from working in their new organic garden. Before, they'd never had time for Jet Skis or tending heirloom tomatoes and pole beans. Admittedly, they had a lot to learn. One of their first lessons was the need for a fence to keep out the free-range deer that also lived around the lake.

They pushed and rocked the Jet Ski off its little dock at water's edge. The engine started on the first try. He drove. She settled herself onto the elongated passenger seat. Along the way he swerved to dodge logs and shallow, muddy patches. He thought his vision seemed sharper with the new blue blocker aviators he had bought online. With each unexpected swerve, she startled, as if she might lose her balance and tumble off. Her arms cinched his waist like a belt.

When they hit rogue waves and landed hard, she leaned in, close to his ear, mouthing their new safe words over the roar of engine and Prine. "Bird bones," she said, their prearranged signal to slow down, a reminder of the brittle realities chasing them. She breathed his familiar scent, and the sight of the glinting silver threading his temples made her snug up, closer, skintight, holding on for their dear lives. In that moment, she sensed the rush of a world passing with fierce velocity. She opened her eyes just as they turned west, directly into the sun, and she swore it felt like flying.

Sherrell R. Wigal

Porch Pinings

I would like to hear
my father, whistling
on Sunday afternoons
as he putters with wrenches,
grease guns, ball-peen hammers.

I would like to hear
the rev of a '57 Chevy,
talk of Glasspack mufflers,
that sudden top-pop
of a long neck Stroh's.

I would like to hear
summer whippoorwill.
That one who calls
on full moon nights
up the Steele Hollow of my youth.

I would like to hear
someone in the kitchen,
clank of pots, clink of glasses,
a voice calling me to supper.

Sherrell R. Wigal

two days past full moon
I have been saying goodbye
since my arrival

Sherrell R. Wigal

Fermata

There is one pause,
      a spontaneous moment,
when evening lays itself down.

      Wind holds its breath.
      Birds settle—silence their songs.
      Animals pause.
      Long out-breath by grasses.

Then,
      a blue inhale,
      tenderness of evening slips in on cooler air.

Quiet night approaches.
      Hermit Thrush rushes into song.
      Doe and fawn rise in meadows.
      Snakes slide home.
      Dusk pulls near.

Patient on the porch
      I wait alone for the moment

my body relaxes,
      skin marries air.

Kari Gunter-Seymour
Pointed Toes & Hand Woven Muslin

Susan Truxell Sauter

Playing By Ear

One day your song is nearly played through,
and you don't know the way into winter.

A few plain sparrows and unconcerned juncos
softly flit and twitter as you pull spent plants.

You watch the season's last hornworm feed,
leave it in a slow-die on the uprooted vine,

succor waning, like mine. I uproot too, return
my water monitor kit, done with the twisted ankle risk

or broken bone alone on some creekbank.
Human bones become hole-shot

while birds hatch with hollow bones for lighter flight.
I volunteered to feed injured owls, fledgling warblers too,

change water, clean cages but decades of over-doing
deny any more from my aching body.

What guidance can I find for this Diminish,
the how-to and when? My radar waits

for time-of-life signals—day length, degree-days,
when to shed parts of myself.

I might try torpor, how hummingbirds conserve energy in migration
though I won't go far in miles—perhaps a length in years.

I pick up my flute, play along to a kd lang song I've never heard.
The music played—rhythm, emotion, the full gather—

lives inside my arms, sound brain-signaled at my ear,
releases, in a mix of breath and fingertip-press on silver keys.

Playing by ear the body knows what to do—

I hear birds sing and kd's words fly and I
don't know how this goes. *

     Calling All Angels by kd lang

Susan Truxell Sauter

Liturgy of Half-Brother

I travel with Half-Brother, my innocent.
Music swells in the car.
From his mouth come words.
At the refrain we repeat together
as we have done before
from our favorite Guster song
    You're my satellite,
    Riding with me tonight.

On Ohio roads, inside the vehicle,
the one with West Virginia plates
our hallowed space—
the Church of Half-Brother/Half-Sister.
The passenger seat is full of him,
long legs bent tight and high,
his sacred garments donned:
sports team coat, sports team hat—a Bills'
ball cap or Buckeyes' knit pull-down
and Browns' gloves for cold.

    COVID has kept us separate—
    so too have the winter seasons. Until we congregate
in one space again, we pray to the same good-travel saint,
    to the virus variant and its color-coded maps,
and to mental health gods neither one of us understand.

Jessica Manack

The Ring Bearers

—for Joseph Hall, 1845-1908

Joseph strode deep into the woods.
He did every day—raised in them, rich from them—
but this day was different, with Alice gone,

gone forever, yet still there, at rest in the front room.
She had just learned to walk, but the fever
bested her, put her to sleep forever.

And he knew that the other children needed to see
his strength, his faith, even when he could not
be sure of it himself. So it was only in front of

the hemlocks that he wailed, the trees breathing in
his exhalations, his carbon dioxide, to use for sugars,
to add mass, the sum of all that year's inputs.

The rings buried deep trapped his grief
to hold it forever, the cries locked inside
1886, 1887, 1888 when he lost his babies

to typhoid: first Alice, then Hattie, and Bessie,
all gone before the age of three. How wrong
that these unloving monoliths should endure.

But they did, and grew fat on the weeping.
And with the trees Joseph fed his family,
felling the elders to send down the rivers,

down the Clarion, the Ohio, the Mississippi, towns
and houses springing up as quickly as the wood came,
made sturdy from the names of the lost.

Jessica Manack

Highway Lifecycle

The vultures have all day.
They glide above us, above the trees,
smirk at our urgency

and profit from it, as below we do
their dirty work, speed through the streets, lay waste
to nature, pile carcasses on the side of the road.

Paint stripes as if to say: here, you feast,
erase our shame so we may kill again
as you watch from above, keeping our secrets.

Jessica Manack

Miracle Season

The first one was the tights I managed not to snag.
The second, the hairspray that held me together,
taming my brittle, bleached hair: nearly respectable. Except
the lip gloss was too brash, too orangey: my grandmother

was right, though I never admitted it until today,
and it clashed with my braces, rubberbanded red and green.
Getting ready by my mother's makeup mirror set to Evening,
I hadn't yet figured out whether I was a summer or a winter.

Seasons? The only linen we ever wore was White Linen,
Mom spraying liberally enough to cover us all,
even, usually, the fumes surrounding our father.
And that was the next miracle: he'd abstained that night,

no shampoo bottle of whiskey in his waistband.
The ballet called for more, our very best behavior,
a chance for the clumsy to witness perfection.
Perhaps we'd see the dolls and mimic them;

perhaps a flame of grace would be lit within.
Since no one had recently died or married,
since our uncle's cancer had vanished
and we no longer needed to go to church,

we'd had to buy new dress clothes, always
cheap, infrequently used, too soon outgrown.
Oh, we were rich with mysteries we couldn't explain,
gangly but still glimmering, too old now to smile

on command, too old, even, for a smile to be beaten out of us.
But smile we did, in unison, still learning our best features,
trying to make our gawky faces make sense,
hoping the veneer would hold for a night, and, miracle

of miracles, it did, but we didn't get greedy, knew
it wasn't worth asking for more, watched our fate
played out on the stage: in some lives,
one night of magic was all you got.

Neva Bryan

Split

I rest on our back porch's top step and watch my nine-year-old nephew follow our dog around the yard. Twinkle Toes has a red baloney string hanging out of her butthole. Carter's trying to step on the string, but the dog slinks away whenever he gets close to her. This ridiculous dance has been going on for near twenty minutes.

This morning I fried the last of the baloney and made gravy off the grease. While I was feeding Carter his breakfast, Twinkle Toes got into the trash and ate the baloney strings.

I roll my eyes as the kid tries to sneak up on the dog, then I holler at him like I'm a football coach. "Man-to-man coverage! Don't go where she is! Go where she's gonna be!"

He manages to stomp on the string with one of the Nike knock-offs Sis bought him at the flea market. Twinkle Toes jerks away from him, and the red plastic slides right out of her butthole. The stupid dog crawls underneath my sister's piece-of-shit Sunbird to hide.

The grass is tall around the car. Sis parked it when the registration and inspection sticker expired. She hasn't been able to save any money to renew them, so her boyfriend drives her to work.

Carter shrugs and cusses the dog.

"Throw that string away," I order. "Not with your fingers! Use your foot!"

A hand grips my shoulder. Dani, my best friend, grins at me. "Hey, Casey. I've been trying to text you all morning."

"My phone's out of minutes." I grab her arm and pull her down to sit next to me. "You packed yet?"

Dani shakes her head.

We both applied to the University of Virginia, and we both got in. We leave for Charlottesville in a few days.

"How about you?" she asks as she examines her fingernails.

I shrug. "Not much to bring with me. Won't take me long to pack."

Dani pulls her hair out of its ponytail, and the scent of Lemon Pledge rises around her. She cleans houses every weekend. When she wraps the hairband around her fingers, I notice she's chewed her nails ragged.

Carter climbs the steps and slides past us. I remind him to wash his hands when he gets inside.

"Hey," Dani says. "I want to tell you something."

"Mmm-hmm." I'm distracted by an ant making curlicues on the step between my feet. It reminds me of my mom. She used to wander the roads day and night, weaving back and forth across the hardtop. One time she fell into a ditch and just laid there until Sis found her and brought her home.

She ain't been here in a long time. I caught sight of her in line at the dollar store about a month ago, and she waved at me. I pretended like I didn't see her.

The ant weaves this way and that. Finally, I nudge it with the tip of my sandal, and it runs off the edge of the step—stupid bug.

Dani pokes me in the ribs. "Let's go to the rock."

"Okay."

I holler at Carter to stay in the house, then Dani and I cross the backyard to the low fence that separates my house from the river. We jump it and walk through the trees until we reach the riverbank.

The river rolls slowly through here. Once it reaches the edge of town, it splits into two fast-moving streams that move away from each other.

A mossy boulder hugs the riverbank. Dani and I have spent a lot of time on this rock.

When we were in first grade, we used to bring our coloring books here. We'd lay on our stomachs to color while we told each other stories.

The stuff we've brought to the rock has changed over the years. Rusty BB guns to shoot leaves off the trees. Overdue library books. Stolen fingernail polish. Binoculars with one broken lens. Magazines for Dani and books for me.

No people, though. This place is ours.

We climb onto the boulder and plop down on the flattest part of it. The sun is high in the sky now.

"What did you want to tell me?"

Dani's eyebrows draw down until they almost meet in a V. After a second, she says, "I ain't going up to Charlottesville."

I stare at Dani, ready to give her hell for kidding around, but the look on her face tells me she's serious.

"What are you talking about? Of course, you're going. We've been planning this for two years."

We spent hours studying for the SAT and got high scores. We got scholarships and Pell grants. I'm going to major in environmental science. Dani wants to be a nurse.

Here's our plan: We'll move away from this shitty town and never look back.

"Plans change." Dani crosses her arms and hugs herself hard. A milky scar covers her right elbow. She got it when we were kids, riding our bikes in the Piggly Wiggly parking lot. She hit a pothole and tumbled over the handlebars. I never saw so much blood.

Dani rubs the scar and shakes her head. "I've been thinking about it. Ain't no way I'm going to fit in there. I can go to community college here and stay home and still work."

My stomach flip-flops. I swallow hard to keep grease gravy from coming up into my mouth. "I don't want to go up there all by myself. I need you to go with me."

"You'll be fine. You're so smart. The smartest person I know. You don't need me." Dani tries to put her arm around my waist, but I move out of reach.

I cross my arms against my knees and rest my forehead on them. The sun is warm in my hair, making my scalp tingle. Closing my eyes, I listen to the cicadas buzzing around us. The sound makes my teeth ache.

"Casey, don't be mad at me."

"I ain't mad." My voice is muffled, but I can't lift my head. It's heavy with sun and buzz and hurt.

"Anyway, we'll see each other when you come home for breaks. And after we graduate, we'll move in together then. So we'll always be best friends."

When I don't say anything, she sighs. After a few minutes, she gets up and leaves.

Leaning back on my elbows, I run my fingers back and forth across the soft moss. Sunlight shimmers on the river's surface. It makes my eyes water.

I swipe at them with the back of my hand.

I stay on the rock for a long time.

When I get back to the house, Carter says he's hungry. So I give him a Little Debbie Swiss Roll and a Dr. Pepper.

After he gobbles his snack, I lick my thumb and use it to wipe chocolate crumbs off his chin. Then, I park him in front of the TV. "Don't bug me," I tell him.

I grab a two-liter bottle of Hawaiian Punch from the kitchen counter before heading to my bedroom.

I pull clothes from drawers and throw them on the bed. Occasionally I stop to swig some punch. It's warm and so sweet that it makes me sick to my stomach. I drink it anyway, just to have something in my belly.

Packing takes longer than I thought it would. By the time I finish, mellow light fills my bedroom. It's softer than sunlight on water. It don't hurt my eyes.

I perch on the sill of my open window. The sun is behind the treetops now. Sunset clouds trail it, piling on top of each other. They stretch and change as they move across the sky.

It's supper time.

Sis still ain't home.

Linda Parsons

Killing the Bed

I'm putting you out of your misery,
white whale of a bed devouring the room,

killing you not softly but whole hog, a king
no longer ruling with any sort of scepter

or decree lording my peasant heart. I wrestle
you down the hall without homage or allegiance

on bent knee, our marriage threadbare and frayed
until night by night no bitty light seeped

through, until you were biting off the whole
of me—at first unsuspecting, though how

could I see the pieces going, my eyes low
in fealty, my belief in on and on clouding

all contention. I air you out in the shock of sun,
drag you to the gate, to the truck's great maw,

you contraption of metal and sunken springs.
I've fallen head over heels with your replacement:

double bed of carved oak pineapples,
an angel at each poster to bear my soul away.

I sweep my feet across memory's foam,
snowy field of wildest dreams, never nearing

the edge, never bumping up against
any sort of darkness, any rued day.

Linda Parsons

Airing it Out

       I take myself to the sun,
though I was never a child of the sun,
basted with Coppertone like the Sunday bird.
A day in June, I find a crook hidden
from street and neighbors, from the waning
pandemic, aloneness my essential oil
and scent. What do I think I'm doing,
unlatching the garden gate where ivy
twines and clay clots, bare-assed,
my knees flailed to noon, where I peer into
the pelvic doorway—memory of my mother
spread-eagle under the heat lamp to heal
her episiotomy, where they cut my sister out.
My grandmother shushes me away:
You don't need to see that.

       But I do, I need to see
the wound closed and glossy. I need
that sear, that high candescence, to be
other than my mother, regret clamped
inside her walls until they mildewed
for lack of light. I need to be done, scars
and all, on a pallet in my own backyard,
open as linen on the line. The corona
radiates its million degrees, solar flares
burn distances I cannot fathom. After
the long virus winter, how can I be
anything but sun-warm skin and bone
down to my brightening folds,
down to the naked earth.

Tina Parker

Daughter-Mother

I have grown girls
In this body
This ground
Has grown me
My daughter brings the seedling
Home in her backpack
      We have to plant it today
      Today mama or it will die
      And water it
      We have to water it every day

The baby would have been
      A girl
She would have grown
      Tall
Like her sisters
      A sunflower

We dig deep
We water
But the seedling grows
Brown leaves I teach her
To pull them off
And wait for green.

Tina Parker

The Midwife

My bare feet
kick up dust
in the creek bed.
Bone-dry,
this fall
and the air
too thick
to breathe.

The scent leads
me through the dusky dark—
her body's musk
with a hint
of damp leaves

Jonas chops wood,
he can't stop.
I climb the stairs
to her and see
she's holding fast.

You have to let go,
I say it
close to her face.
Forget the wash,
the sheets you'll dirty.
Here stand up,
that's it.
The baby can't come
till you let go.
The pain is a light,
reach for it now.

My hands can't go around,
so I am under her arms
to hold her from behind.
We squat by the window.
Her eyes are gone,
she won't see

the stars so I tell her
It's a clear night.

A moan
and her body knows
to bear down.
Her hands all bone
on the windowsill,
but still she is silent.

You got to go
a little crazy.
Find your anger
and push it out.
Scream now scream
the sickness scream
the dark hole
you push through.

Finally her voice
cuts the night.
The ax drops,
the baby coming out
slick on the sheets.
It's a girl,
and she cries fierce
till their bodies
find each other again.

There is work
to do yet,
but I know
to sit and watch
the baby suckle back
to that first sleep,
to that comfort
we come from
but can never keep.

Stephanie Kendrick

Home For Sale

Don't let the holes in the siding sway you.
This skin is tough, alive,
has made room for birds to nest inside.
Here, you are never without song
that seeps into your dark spots and swells.

Pay no mind to the pipes that drip.
We never held back here, never
allowed the pressure to build.
Just catch it with a bucket
for the flowers you might grow.

Check out these floors, grout cured
with specks of dirt from a first hike,
sand from a trip to Clearwater, the one
with glassblowers, an ocean moon
and what it made us do
in the sketchy motel bathroom.

And I just won't apologize
for the Sharpie masterpieces upstairs,
done with hands that were so small—
the sole reason, to be sure,
for the sky-high property value.

I hope you noticed the absence
of the French doors that once separated rooms—
doors removed by my husband's hands,
and never returned to their hinges.
I am sure you are more adept than we
at installations and separations. Now,

don't let the sounds of the crawlspace stop you.
Ground moles find solace underneath our feet,
mice squeak mystery to the housecats above.
This home has been a playground for all.
And anyway, didn't I tell you
there'd be music?

Stephanie Kendrick

I Guess Now We Know

—For Adam

If he would have had a mid-life crisis
it would've happened at seventeen.

We were Cancers, and he couldn't drive
even though on weekends, he'd man
the wheel of Chelsie's '89 Honda—
the one with the broken headlight
that matched her lazy left eye.

Once, he took a curve too fast,
about went through the laundromat.
They live forever, don't they?
Hondas and laundromats, I mean.
He never got the knack for steering,
the flow of stop and go,
the wiring of it all.

He escaped that summer on a plane.
Landed in Kansas City.
Thrived.

Yesterday he decided to leave again.
Too many curves taken too fast.
Still no knack for steering,
no steady flow of stop and go,
the wiring of him was in control.

They said he opened his door first,
so his cat wouldn't be stuck inside,
so they both could be free.

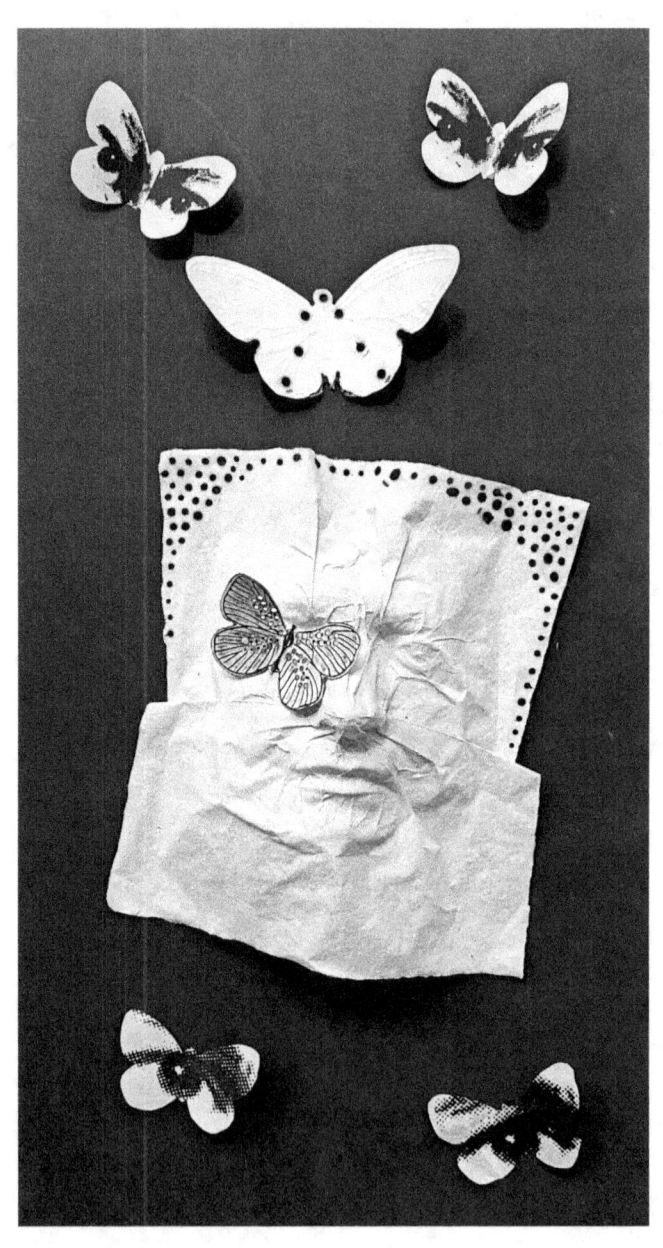

Kathy Guest
Looking for Hope

Shei Sanchez

Prayer for the Equinox

Sunday morning, we amble eastward
   to the rising light. These hills & hollers

of home never tire of ruminant tongues
   & teeth, never tire of their fervent trembling

to pluck supple wafers of honeysuckle, boxelder,
   ash. On this route, the goats and I forage

as family, scenting life with naked wonder, tasting
   its breath. In my mouth, I savor a tender

spicebush leaf— its bitter comfort a panacea
   for living in this world. In my palm, I hold

its red berries like currency for existence.
   On a land bridge, strands of sun pierce

through crowns of buckeye and beech. Is God
   waking me to listen? Telling me to wait for a hymn

in an extant breeze or birdsong? A large burl
   on an old oak snaps me back to days

of a bulging belly, a body unfit for birthing,
   the certainty of disease. Seven years now

since I opened the door of acceptance. Feels
   much longer in my womb. This time of year,

ghosts of motherhood live in marcescent trees,
   in the art & dance of vines, in boot prints pressed

on the earthen clay. Whisper to me your name, child.
   I am chiseling your shape beneath the blue

of our vanished autumn sky. The equinox will soon turn
   & I will, too— another revolution around the sun.

I'll turn & turn until the mud hardens underneath my feet.

Shei Sanchez

Interrogations on Red

How deep does the red of your fire go?
  In syncopated madness, swooning
from ember to ephemeral ember—how hot
  is the heat of your heart? Do you burnish
the fire-pink petals of a catchfly, cup
  the ruby throat of a hummingbird breaking
his solitude in the thrust of spring? Does
  your flame grow on time's wick, reach
the belly of the sun, down into the canthus
  of the Eye of Ra whose early morning
light awakens every dawn?

I burn to know if the crimson
  of *Trifolium incarnatum* sleeps
inside the clovers' inflorescence, flirts
  with bees til noon's yawn. Does
your voice whisper like the velvet petal
  of a pawpaw tree's flower, or soothe
like clay in a sculptor's hands? Can you
  taste death's pigment that lingers
on the bitter side of your tongue, carry
  life within the marrow of man's kind?

To me, you are more than just a color
  living at the long end of light. More
than a scatter of clouds at the close of day.

To the bullfighter, you are vehicle
  and ferment to her bull.
To the Renaissance painter, a lover
  for his blue to conjure violet.
To the blood moon, a cloak
  of fire cradling her totality.

Shei Sanchez

Letter for Home

You smelled of mid-autumn dew, a burnt ochre swirled
in the wet mouth of morning. The aging acer ached
toward you, almost prostrate, as you danced against
the waning light of rose, peach, apricot. I listened
to your waltz as my skin puckered beneath thin layers
of fabric: a raiment jeweled with heat, the Mekong, buds
of a leelawadee. Metal & exhaust wafted from my pores,
the syncopated streets of Bangkok still baked into my bones.
You welcomed me anyway, to a new home, unhurried
with each dawn & dusk, each frost & flower that followed—
even as I stumbled upon you, stepped over every family
of burdock, moss, cinnamon fern growing on you. Each
footprint on your body, an imprint on mine. Even when
illness felled my own body, you nurtured that part of me
that surrendered, breathed fire into it, let it burn
until I stood alive again. Eight years close to the day
you took me in, I still smell your dew. I still hear you
dancing, the maple rooting me to your song.

Susan Powers

Finding Blue (Song)

Words still linger in the air
Up there in the blue
Going where the air is thin
That's what you chose to do

And you never had the glory
To be the queen of pop
You just have to keep on moving
You can never stop

You've got
Your finger on the pulse
Reaching for another source

But these forms are all around us
It happens everyday
Anonymous still lingers
Turning blue to gray

Don't feel sorry for me
Remember we were free
I might have lost you forever
But that could never be.

Susan Powers

Fiddler's Wake (Song)

Grandpa was a fiddle player
Chew your tobacco and spit your juice
Was a teacher and a farmer
Could of raised Cain but it was no use
Down at the dance where the wine was flowing
Had some sips and he'd start bowing

Euphoria
Setting those fields on fire
Euphoria
Elizabeth and the babies crying
Euphoria
We used live in a state of grace
Euphoria
Down in the barn at the fiddler's wake

Red is the rose and green is the brier
Sing in the choir till your lungs get higher
Preacher tells a different story
If we ride this train we are bound for glory
Down at the dance where the wine was flowing
Had some sips and he'd start bowing

Save all your money save all you got
And you'll always have money in your old tobacco box

Cat Pleska

Drive!

Opal Pearl wanted to learn to drive. Her sister's former boyfriend owned a car, and since he was a free man, Opal thought he might be the one for her. She waited by the road one hot summer day, nervously smoothing down her dress. Here he came down out of the holler in his Model T, a cloud of dust billowing out behind.

She was a woman of her time. Her family came from the country, but for a short time her father ran a butcher shop, and they lived in a town of 5,000 trendy souls. She learned about suffrage and found the hem lengths above the knee exciting. She'd bobbed her thick black hair to angle along her jaw line. That day, beside the road, life's possibilities bubbled up in her mind, and the adventures she'd have if only she could drive. Where exactly she'd drive to remained vague. Buzzing around, girlfriends along for the ride, meant freedom, something most modern women in the Roaring Twenties wanted.

The driver stopped and shouted for her to "Hop in!" She wasted no time climbing in on the passenger's side, eyeing the steering wheel and then the man.

They courted and Opal Pearl married her driving teacher. Six children later, with the right to vote, and a home to care for, she drove her husband to the bootleggers on Sunday so he wouldn't be out on the road driving drunk. She drove to the grocery store, with me, her granddaughter, in the back of the truck leaning way over to watch the tires spin around on the pavement. The wind curled up against the cab of the pickup and blew my hair straight up. Opal Pearl kept her head pointed forward, smoked cigarettes that she flipped out the open window and sometimes landed in the bed of the truck near me.

Once, she drove me and a couple cousins all the way up into the mountains to a family camp. That hot and humid night she danced around the kitchen to *Hot Town, Summer in the City* on the radio, and I remember her laugh when she told a story. I asked her once if she thought about what life would be like if she'd not married my grandfather. She said, "Well, I wouldna had your daddy and there wouldn't be no you." She chuckled. Then she grew serious for a second and said, "I 'spect I'd be married to a movie star and live in a big house. And we'd travel. I'd be driving, wherever I wanted to go."

Every day, she cooked and cleaned, took a punch or two in the ribs when my grandfather was drunker than drunk. Her hair turned salt and pepper but was as thick as ever. She shifted gears in the truck like she was born to race at NASCAR. When she was driving, her eyes never left the road.

***

Doris Jean didn't drive when she was a teen. There was no money, hardly any for food or clothes. She quit school after the tenth grade to work in a dime store. She walked to her job and one day met a man who looked like Robert Mitchum and had a swagger like James Dean. His cool car didn't hurt—a 1951 Desoto—his father's she found out later. He'd take beautiful blue-eyed, dark-haired movie-star-looking Doris Jean for long drives, the windows down, her hand skimming the air as they traveled past the homes, the businesses and into the West Virginia hills, going faster and faster.

My movie-star-handsome dad, just out of the Korean War, persuaded Mom to marry him and picked her up for the nuptials in that same De Soto. By this time, the freedom women expected had turned into a house with a white picket fence, children, two cars in the garage, all a housewife could want.

One night while driving drunk Dad fell asleep behind the wheel and hit someone head on. The authorities took his license for 10 years, and he was allowed only to drive to work. He forbade Mom to drive, or to get her license. "You're too nervous. You'd wreck," he told her over and over. We all knew the real reason was that he had to pay high risk insurance. One claim on either of his cars, even for a small dent that wasn't her fault, and he'd be parked for a long time.

Mom's sister, Norma, took her to the store, to yard sales, to visit their siblings. Wearing her freshly-pressed, creased jeans with her hair perfectly coiffed, she sat primly and waited, sometimes half a day, for Norma to pick her up. The clock ticked. She'd call her. Where are you, she'd ask. "Jean, I'm just getting in the shower," her tired-of-chauffeuring sister always said. "Why don't you get your license?" But Jean eventually did get her license; her friend Dorothy took her. Mom had snuck Dad's second car out for the test.

But Doris Jean grew more and more fearful of driving as the years passed, as my dad warned her constantly, "You don't have the nerves to drive," but she faithfully renewed her license each year in case that day came when she could get behind the wheel and drive. She wanted to go to classes to earn her GED. Mom thought a high school diploma might help her get a job. Maybe then Dad would let her drive their second car because she could pay the insurance on it. She signed up but then decided it was pointless to get the GED. I begged her to do so; I promised to help with lessons. No, she shook her head at me. Dad's constant braking on her dreams had sunk in too far.

A few times, while Dad was at work, Mom, feeling strong, grabbed the extra set of keys. Getting in their sedan, she slipped it into drive and eased it down the driveway. She then put it in reverse and backed back up the driveway. Getting out of the car, she checked that she parked it exactly where he'd left it, down to the bent leaf, the slight indent in the gravel. Once, she sneaked out and drove all the way to the post office. I saw her when she returned. I asked her, "Mom, why are you sweating so much?"

Her blue eyes were wide, bright. When Dad came home from work, he said to her, "I stopped by the post office. No mail."

"Is that so?" she said.

***

There was never any question that when I came of age I would drive— we'd come a long way, baby! It was the 70s! I cut my teeth on the first wave of feminism, but it was baby steps. Like many young women then an interest in a guy to date meant he had to have a car—to take us to the drive-in, to eat, the rock concerts, the bowling alley, to buzz the highway in front of friends, to park on some dark lane.

I married at 19, my wedding dress a good six inches above my knees. I refused to allow the preacher to use the word "obey" in our vows. He almost refused to marry us.

I spent thirty-five years on the passenger side with a husband who was a distracted driver. I had to call his attention back to the road a million times. He also seemed averse to stopping in a timely fashion. My knuckles turned white all the time from clutching the door rest. Once, we had a Honda Civic that had a thin floor. A rod that came across the width of the car underneath connected the brakes. I discovered it was sensitive to my anxious foot pressing hard down on the floorboard from the passenger side.

"What the hell," he said. "What's causing the car to slow? I'll have to take it to the garage."

"I suppose so," I said.

Over and over I asked myself why I did not challenge him. Even now any car on the road, with a man and a woman in it, guess who's behind the wheel? I didn't know any of my friends questioning this assumption. It was a long time before my courage went into overdrive.

Of course, I could drive anywhere in our second car by myself: to the store, belly dancing lessons, taking our daughter to school, and to work at a craft shop. Eventually, I drove to college, to graduate school, then I drove all the way to Baltimore for my Master of Fine Arts classes. My engines were revving.

I taught college for nearly 15 years and saved my money. Then one day I realized I could buy my own car: a brand new Subaru. I drove it off the dealership's show room floor with only 4 miles on the odometer. I named my car Bluebell and deeply inhaled that new car smell. I owed no one for this long-needed freedom: except the loan company.

I wanted my name only on the registration, but my husband was afraid there'd be legal problems, even though our reciprocal wills say if I die before him he gets my clothes, my books, my cats, all that I've ever written, and my car. Yet, I caved, let him include his name. But I insisted I was always the driver. He wasn't happy, but he got used to it.

My sweet car reached ten years old and 202,000 miles. I saw a photo of the new car I wanted. A cherry red SUV with a back-up camera, lane warning lights and chimes and all kinds of bells and whistles. This time, my name is the only one on the registration.

***

Every time I get behind the wheel, the ghostly presences of Opal Pearl and Doris Jean hoot at me from the backseat like the free-spirited duo Thelma and Louise. "Put the pedal to the metal, Cat!"

I holler back, "That's right, ladies! This stretch of highway is for us. And it's endless."

Rhonda Pettit

Notes from an Underground Angel

i.

Up from the dark of library microfilm
Up from the stumps and stones of deeds
Up from the shades and bottoms of the past
Cresting the ridge into late-day sun, I drive by

A white horse grazing in the green grass beside a yellow house

The rich black asphalt and the road lines fresh
The tires now strum to the rhythms of the ridge-top
On either side the land rocks steeply down to pasture

A white horse grazing in the green grass beside a yellow house

Through the blur of roadside barns missing planks and shingles
Through the glare of oncoming cars and shuddering trucks

A white horse grazing in the green grass beside a yellow house

Heading north, heading home, out of fact, into vision, in my mind

A white horse grazes in the green grass beside a yellow house

ii.

Not the apocalypse
Not the good knight or the bad ones
Not the naked lady long in the hair

Not the plow
Not the show
Not the muse

Not the glue factory
Not the dog food
Not the unicorn

Not the chariot, not the war
Not the general, not the god
Not the rodeo, not the track

Nothing to do with myth or madness
Not the monument
Not me.

Just a white horse with nothing to do
but graze the green grass
beside the yellow house
as I happen to pass by.

iii.

The stark contrast
a white horse luminous
among those deep and sonorous
colors
without conflict.

Their susurrus.

iv.

It could have been bay, gray, or midnight,
stallion, gelding, mare.

Now every horse I see, wherever it stands,
is this horse:

the green grass, the yellow house, the blue sky, the ridge road
rush to recreate this vision,
its utterance,

and together we ride.

Rhonda Pettit

Stopped at a Crossing

I am up front and patient enough
to watch and enjoy

as the truncated body of train lumbers
south, rumbas a bit

the plastic and metal of my Honda
and my nerves.

Like the seventeen-year brood it seems
it will never end

and there they are: impatient cicadas
trying to anyway

cross the tracks, rising but not high
enough, bumping

into tanker cars of corn syrup and
molten sulfur,

dropping back, rising again, clearing
the hoppers

and flatbeds. They have found their rhythm,
their timing for clearing

the machine in their garden of now, of necessity,
of meeting and mating

on the other side of the tracks with no daddy's curse
or a momma's boo-hoo, then

BAM! the tri-level autoracks arrive and the soft
thump of failure

spins them down again. This is too much, this
and the birds, too,

chasing them, eating them alive. I briefly ache
for them, long for

a kinder crossing for all of us, but the gates lift,
the train delivering

its goods & murders finished with us for now,
the flashing lights,

red as a cicada's eyes, blink off and off I go,
off we all go,

Bruegheling beyond the failure of flight, of art
as if love didn't matter.

Randi Ward
Quain't

Lynette Ford

Haint

She thought she heard footfall so soft it was a dream
like sheer curtain torn and dancing
dark fairy wing zuzzing
a sound lost in cobwebs
in dusty corners
in memory in moonlight
like someone waving away a thought
just as she opened the door.
She thought she saw
something of shadow
between the ticks of twilight
there
no there
yes someone
like bits of dust
shimmering out of frame
near the rim of her eye.

Lynette Ford

All Ourselves and One

Africa's memory speaks from Appalachian hill
old earth the Grandmother of Mother Africa
coal here was born there
where traces of now began as dreams
the promise of diamonds hidden in land massed as
the core of continents
rifts and breaks and slow collisions celebrated
the World's Grandmother
When we walk the Appalachian Trail
we touch earth that was Africa
memory set in stone
eons of heritage
that time
once
when the continents were one
rifts and breaks and slow collisions
transformations and separations
Grandmother's heart quivering shuddering
shaping mountains
Grandmother's tears flowing forming
rendering criks runs rivers oceans
in time before time
ancestral elevations of sacred homeland
are soft blue-shadowed mountains
low green hills
some misformed and misinformed
by human minds and hands
yet still they whisper
the labor of their birth
the history bleached nearly white except for the coal
Once these mountains were
the edge of Africa
Stand here now and know these hills
are still
Our Blessed Grandmother
She who waits here to uplift us
Spirit of that place of birthing beyond generations
We who are Affrilachia must speak testaments
stories formed in the Soul of the Grandmother of

Mother Africa
We may be ignored by others
but we are not forgotten by the earth
We must stand here now
all ourselves and one
Africa's memory speaks from Appalachian hill

Kory Wells

Insomnia Ritual

—For Darnell and Amie

Who yet returns to walk a woman's rooms —James Dickey

I haven't washed the sheets since
        she slept on them
which is   and is not   a commentary on my
        housekeeping—
it's been so many months
                I've lost track and

no one but me has needed that bed
        on occasion
like tonight
        when I bleary my way upstairs
pretending to be a guest
                pretending

to be a woman who sleeps
        in the night. What comfort
to imagine my friend here
        resting
            reading aloud
her bowed vowels

        an old fiddle tune.
What solace,
my skin against thin cotton where
        her skin
      left the thinnest elixir of
dander and oil.   Salt and sweat and cells—

        every night's a leaching away,
a wearing down.   Today the nurse called
        to say the spot in my breast
           has grown.
I'd like to tell you I'm being brave,
        but I'm barely managing

              philosophical   which is to say
my mind's stitching and backstitching
          a crazy patchwork—
we all have our
        into every life a little
          why me   must fall.

I could smother   under this quilt
        of clichés   but for my friend
her voice   an untroubling I repeat: Let me
        be awake.   Let me toss and turn
                  my fears into fortune
cookies I nightstand   in a porcelain bowl.

Let me be the old woman
                  who every night rises
        and empties her closet   tossing aside
everything but an old trench coat
she buttons and belts
                  and wears back to bed.

Kory Wells

When You Said for Richer or Poorer

Trouble was only a theory
far in the future, a thorn
deep under the stem

of ever-after. But now,
on the way home
from your honeymoon,

he slips into your hand
a crystal saltshaker
lifted from the dining room's

white linen and hush.
You wonder, for a thin breath,
if there will be repercussions.

Cops? A collection agency?
No. This is such a small
loss, an elegant choice.

The thought soothes
the quick prick of complicity,
but beneath your breastbone

a mean-eyed jay begins
to build its sharded nest.
And now your husband's saying

the line between
good and bad is very
fine. He's saying

don't look at me
that way. Nipped, you
do not hold his gaze.

You study your palm,
weighted fortune in hand:
cut and polished. Grit and lead.

Alyson Annette Eshelman
Seeking Wisdom

Lois Spencer

A Different Kind of Poor

Hard as it was to imagine people living with less worldly treasure than we had, one sultry August afternoon in 1954, I encountered just such a family. On the heels of that discovery came two additional lessons that would stick with me and influence the person I became.

My paternal grandmother's brother Albert lived in the hills out back of Philo, Ohio, and could have been the prototype of grisly old hillbilly. And even though he kept no livestock and raised no crops, his raw-boned wife, Mamie, carried all the labors of farm wife on her stooped shoulders. Mom, who had little use for Albert's sister—her mother-in-law—had taken a liking to Mamie and her daughter Bernice. At fifteen, Bernice had given birth to a baby boy whose father conveniently ducked out of the picture before his spit-and-image son appeared on the scene. Now, at twenty, Bernice had zero prospects for self-support or marriage and—had it been numerically possible—even less self-confidence.

Ready to begin her senior year, my sister Barbara had finally lost her waif-like thinness and acquired a nicely-rounded figure. Much of the clothing she had purchased through Aid to Dependent Children no longer fit but was way too nice for the ragbag. Saving it for me would have been ludicrous considering the ten years' age difference between us. Mom immediately thought of Bernice, who'd remained as skinny as a broom. So Barbara carefully packed the out-grown pieces in brown grocery sacks, and in the oppressive heat, the three of us ventured out to the Jenkins property.

No breeze at all stirred the ancient oaks shielding the weather-worn farmhouse as Mother shifted down and turned into the driveway. We saw Albert on the front porch, winding in a new wad of Mail Pouch, flannel shirt and bib overalls defying the heat index. Dangling his legs over the porch edge sat Bernice's Tommy, red hair glowing as if lit from inside, freckles in sharp relief against the white skin.

The whine of the Plymouth's engine and the rattle of cinders against its fenders brought Mamie and Bernice to the kitchen door sweat-streaked, lank tendrils of hair clinging to their faces. Heat from the kitchen flooded toward us as we approached the door, seeking to dissolve itself into the comparative coolness of August shade.

A big pot of tomatoes bubbled front and center on the coal and wood range. On the right hand side, away from the firebox, sat a row of Mason jars upside down on a grimy dishtowel. Custom demanded that Mom join in the kitchen work. Custom also sent Bernice to fetch fresh water from the well and offer us a drink while Mamie ladled each jar full and topped it with one of the flats floating in water. Mother took the hot jar from Mamie, wrapped it in her apron, and twisted the metal ring tight enough to ensure a seal.

With nothing else to do, I took in the kitchen, at eight years old noticing details that I hadn't before. Soot darkened the ceiling and wall nearest the cook stove, and the bare board floor sagged toward the middle of the room. Dust-streaked windows were propped up with sticks, but curtains hung as motionless as the trees outside. Furnishings consisted of a wobbly wooden table and chairs, some backless; a kitchen cupboard that used to be white; and a washstand positioned beneath a wavy mirror. Nowhere could I see an ice-box, and my tepid jar of water begged for a sliver of ice. I knew better than to ask; my sister's hand—a vice with fingernails—awaited the chance to clamp my wrist.

While we didn't have a refrigerator at our house, we stocked an ice box with a huge, frozen rectangle from the ice house at least once a week. To prolong the precious cold, we took the car on days like this and the ice man quickly transferred the block to the towel-lined trunk. If the weather was cool, we pulled the ice block home in my wagon. I hung at the open door and breathed in the cold, steamy air smelling of closed space and metal.

Now, Mom was never a stellar housekeeper, and she was the first to admit it, but she was meticulous about the kitchen. Hot, sudsy water in an oval dish pan brought the squeak to her dishes even before they were scalded with boiling water from the teakettle. Dishtowels were hung to dry on hinged wooden dowels. By contrast, in Mamie's kitchen, the dishwater had formed a scum and the dishtowel in Mom's hand was sprinkled with mildew. A sour staleness permeated the breathless, muggy atmosphere; from that day to this, I have associated that smell with a kind of poverty as different from ours as night from day.

After the women had finished the tomatoes, we walked through shaded rooms and joined Albert on the front porch. He acknowledged our presence with a nod and then shot a streak of tobacco juice into the dry stalks of day lilies skirting the porch. Tommy scurried to Bernice and buried his face in her apron, but Mamie pulled him into her lap and gestured Bernice and Barbara into the front room while I wondered why we hadn't just dropped off the hand-me-downs and headed back to Duncan Falls.

I was beyond surprise when Barbara grabbed my hand and included me in the business of girls and clothes and I saw the anticipation burn two r red spots in Bernice's cheeks as she stripped down to a slip translucent from wear and washboard. She tried on each garment as Barbara handed it to her, turning this way and that to pick up her reflection in the glass door of an ancient, loose-jointed secretary, smiling as Barbara nodded approval and helped with fasteners.

Until then, the human need for dignity and respect had evaded me. But watching my sister's grace in giving introduced me to the day's third and most haunting lesson. What people have or don't have, where or how they live are minor details. The way we choose to treat them is of true consequence.

Jennifer Hambrick

Refashioned

—after a dress by an unknown maker and remade
c.1840 by Mary Slade Stevenson

When she's 15, she walks down the aisle,
floorboards creaking as her Oxford bow pumps

carry her past pews packed with townsfolk sizing
up her propriety. The air hangs heavy with truth.

She is laced and cottoned, wildflowers flocked
into the muslin that cinches her waist to a prim

vanishing point. The dress is heaven hued before it
fades nearly white from wear to church and cotillions,

where whispers of dowry slip around the sidelines.
A few pennies each month, saved for two years,

buys the fabric. It's been a while since she's grown,
so her mother takes out the scissors and thread,

pumps the treadle, and sews her daughter's future
on the bias. An oblong box sits today on a cabinet

full of folders stuffed with yellowed tax returns.
My grandmother makes the box from the cardboard

of a bolt of fabric, covers it with scraps of white
polyester with a windowpane pattern woven

into its warp. Pearl-tipped pins secure a corsage of red
satin roses and green velveteen leaves to the top,

and when it opens, I am 15 and wearing the dress
my mother made from that cloth and my date pins

the corsage over my left collar bone and his brown wool
jacket prickles strong against my fingertips in the cool

of autumn and the scent of aftershave that end a few
weeks later, after the homecoming dance leaves in a swirl

of its own stardust. My teenaged hands fumbled with
the lose threads of that frayed love, its thin scraps now

shaped by years and my much wiser foremothers who,
seamed into their own lives, saw my future open as a lid.

Jennifer Hambrick

Raw Edge

—after Andrea Myers' fabric sculpture Zig Zagged

Everything blows up in a cosmic second
and tears a life to rags and remnants,
leaving scraps of what had been a person

standing firm in the firmament floating
in a sea of chaos and confusion.
War widows bring their husbands' suits

to my grandmother, who makes her pittance
trimming trousers into skirts, curving
boxy jackets to hourglass figures

new to punching timeclocks in a place
in every way so far from home. Bombs
and bloodshed blister the walls of domestic

tranquility, gouge out a no-woman's-land
where every paycheck is a size too small
and hierarchy shears woman from onion skin

and pins her in place on futile fabric.
Wallflower, step forward and be
cut off at the knees, be hemmed in,

the mouth of your heart sewn shut
by surge after surge of holes punched
through the skin of your dignity. And all

the shreds of who you might have been
stitched together by mismatching thread
so taut it frays the mind to think about it.

The world is not round, it is angled.
It is not smooth, it elbows through air
and ether like fins slicing waves into sea

glass, wake healing only until the next seam
sears through. The world rewards those
tailored to its pattern, makes them light

their own orange flames that burn
then fade beyond the horizon line basted
in the space between what could be and what is.

Barbara Costas Biggs

I Had a Good Time Once, Not Too Long Ago

but today I have the heaviness, I'm made hopeless
by the blanket of gray clouds that have swaddled
the sky for a week. The heaviness is the sky, but it is also
my chest and my back; my chest wanting to take
a break from the reflexive in and out, my back
wishing for wings to carry me high, up and away,
looking out for other travelers below.
I'm listening for anything that will break
me of this stupor—the scream of a cyclone,
the squeak of the white-tailed chipmunk
who lives in the stone wall outside my kitchen window.
The sound of my children not bickering.
I had a good time once, not too long ago, and like
in the movie, after it moves back to black and white,
I want to say *and you were there, and you and you*
while someone presses the cold cloth to my forehead.

Barbara Costas Biggs

Ex-Lover Speaks of Appalachia

My second year in Tucson, the town next to my hometown flooded, made CNN, people canoeing down 52, standing on top of their cars. I showed my roommates, telling them I knew that carry-out, knew that intersection. When I met the boy I was sleeping with, he laughed when I said the word "duvet." I said it right, I used it correctly. He thought it was funny that an Appalachian girl knew what a duvet was, maybe even had the audacity to own a duvet. He told me a story about his mother, a nurse who grew into a politician's wife, learning about hill people being tended to by doctors on horseback. He told me like it was yesterday. Like it was my story. Like I got my meningitis vaccine from a man sitting in a saddle, savior to us all.

Barbara Costas Biggs

What My Mourning Looks Like Six Years Later

Today is the day I set aside for you, every year. I mourn
you this year with a kitchen towel thrown over
my shoulder because you said that's that way real
chefs do it. I mourn you with an apron on. I mourn you
by peeling the carrots, springing for actual
guanciale, not just thick-cut bacon. I mourn you
with the Rancho Gordo beans that are soaking. I mourn
you not with cabernet, but with pinot noir because I prefer
it, and I don't think you'd care.   I mourn
you six years later, reminded again that I know every
word to *Helplessly Hoping*. I listen loudly, so loudly
that my son asks what I'm doing. I mourn you
with if it's too loud, you're too old.
When I write a poem about you, there is always music.

Sheila Carter-Jones

Boy

Other teachers think he is strange. It isn't
his almond-colored skin. It is his eyes.
They are blue as if the ocean is in him and
the water has risen up past his lids into his
pupils. His eyes are placid. The calmness
makes teachers question. They want to know
how this ocean happened. It is odd. Makes
them uncomfortable. Doesn't make sense.
He isn't what they expect. Not mean. Not
loud. Or, a smart aleck. It would be easier
to label him a troublemaker if he had regular
eyes. Remove him from their discomfort.
They would feel less threatened by the way
his body in motion appears to be still. He is
just a boy with a soft voice. When he makes
comments or answers questions in class his
eyes are words and his voice is held back by
a blush. When his mouth swells into a smile
his cheeks puff up as if to make his eyes two,
distant, blue suns rising together and
scattering light. Other teachers ask over and
over if I can believe such a thing as a brown
boy with blue eyes. I say, Yes, I see him. I see
how he dreams in his Air Jordans. How his
voice carries him up before his body is a
bubble bursting. Before other teachers insist,
he will never be anything. I wish they could
have seen him beyond their horizon. How he
wouldn't become a negative statistic but
graduate from high school as a promise with
a scholarship. How he would become an
engineer, outstanding employee and featured
as a fine example. See his wife, a scientist, and
their baby born with a smile. How he works
fulltime, has his own side business clearing
weeds, landscaping, and making way for
planting seeds. And, the young boys he hires
are quiet. They blush too.

Sheila Carter-Jones

Elegy—Book of 3 Samuel III

Verse 1. Sailor Sam

Old seaman sailing across. Your well-worn
watch-cap, now a deeper blue, holds down
a spray of speckled gray hair uncertain as
perceiving a body in misty morning fog.

Of all faraway lands traveled, coming home
to three alleys and the small house on
the turn of a bend was the last stop—three
rooms and two wobbly wooden planks to
the toilet.

Seventeen feet from the yard, a utility pole
with a street light hanging was base for night
games and the seeker hunted as you lay
hidden between rows of corn stalks.

Your skin blended with the black of summer
nights until you leaped like a stalk yanked
from its roots and nearly fooled the moon.

A body without substance clothed in t-shirt
and tan shorts ran to touch base like a ghost
whirly-gigged in heated waves of summer. It
was full speed ahead straight into the knotted
trunk of the crab-apple tree.

When you came to, you swore to God the tree
had moved and even crossed your heart as a
spot above your brow began to swell. It took
days for the dark inside your head to clear.

And, it would be years from lying flat out in
night dew that your eyes shimmered again
with a certain kind of starlight.

Verse 2. Sailing

Deer Creek never looked so long as forever from
the bridge that Saturday in late March. How
different the sun mirroring its own light. Nothing
like split-second silver splashes of brilliance
emanating from the body of a rainbow trout's
afterglow. Back when our brown skin glistened
too, we pinched our noses between thumb and
forefinger, the other hand raised to the sky as we
played baptism, screamed hallelujah and slipped
to the underworld.

You are still with us in the urn your Ex carries to
the bridge where we gather and surround her. It is
so cold we shiver as the wind cuts gracefully like
a widow's hand. We stand on the bridge unsure if
its newness will hold us as when one after another,
and all day summer after summer, we cannon-balled
from its top before we learned to dive and enter
the water seamlessly to be in oneness as if a fish,
or tadpole, or minnow.

We stand now, humbled and ice-cheeked knowing
it all has come to this moment of ash and bits of
bone. She pours a stream as the wind lends a push
until you get your footing. When you have skipped
way down by the trestle and barely a see-through
whisp, daredevil Turk says, There goes Sammy, and
we all laugh at loss like we always do, as if laughter
is how we learned to keep ourselves from sinking.

Verse 3. Two Roses

I let two dried roses stand for Sammy's life and
life again. One has bloomed and spread its stiff
purple-crimson like a fan church ladies unfurl to
create small pockets of fresh breath. Wilted leaves
hold brittle petals as if to balance the flower in an
arthritic tangle of dry-green. So deep and still
the beauty, even prickly thorns have not lost their
sharpness. Their poignant way of stating
the unknowable—how their pricks still draw blood

until it drips as a childhood pact between two
friends smearing red, flesh to flesh—to always.

The other rose I keep has the same purple-crimson
complexion. It has not opened. The leaves do not
hold the velvety bulge of body close. They flair as
if to give room for the promise of growth like a
woman plumps with child. From deep inside layered
petals, as if from a little lump of flesh, comes a faint
fragrance of spring. And, the slender curve of stem
is feminine in appearance.

In a brief moment of turning what has not yet
matured in light, I get a glimpse of how Sammy
will return, slim, with an almost black toughness.
Mid-stem an ancient-green leaf is curled like
a hand on the hip—daring and sassy.

KB Ballentine

Leafspear of Light

From a graveyard of pines
a towhee trills, one voice box gliding
into the second, an answer farther in the woods.

I might imagine them dreaming
as silhouettes of dogwood branches lace
the forest floor, what's left of last winter's storms.

Clouds pebble the sky, almost glued
to an excruciating blue. March grumbled in,
now a brilliance of forsythia and redbud.

Today we too can sing out of our losses,
take the shadows for what they are—
ephemeral darkness—no weight, no substance.
                                             Only stardust.

KB Ballentine

The Almost Invisible

There's mystery in gray skies—
    a sanctuary in the mist,
the softness of dove wings,
    the luminescence of sea pearls
beckoning from coral and sand.
    Between music and pain,
it's a shade that wanders
    in wind, cloud, and storm,
tastes like sleep and ink,
    dreams lost in fog
and hydrangeas' chalk-white petals.
    Gray slips like smoke
into the space between passion
    and heartbreak, pebbles
spilling from the tip of the tongue.

KB Ballentine

Heart, Full of Seed

Wind thrashes the oaks, scatters acorns
against the metal roof where squirrels will feast.
This room, warm and snug, embraces me.
Though the sun has risen and blues the sky,
frost veils the cars, the yard, my heart.
So many years I shaped you as the villain,
but I want to let that go.

A splinter moon sets my mind wandering.
Do you remember finding me on that midnight trail
when the rescue searchers couldn't?
How you even brought a thermos of hot tea
and pulled socks from your pocket? You were the light
I knew would shine. And you shattered me.

But the shards I have gathered are trimmed in gold—
the edges of every scar shimmering with wisdom,
even a kind of peace. Blow, wind. Go ahead
and toss the branches. Blow. Drop the loose,
the weak, the rotten things and watch me
                                        turn them into gifts.

CONTRIBUTOR BIOS:

Neema Avashia is the daughter of Indian immigrants. She was born and raised in southern West Virginia, but now lives in the city of Boston, where she works as an educator. Her first book, *Another Appalachia: Coming Up Queer and Indian in a Mountain Place*, was published by WVU Press in March of 2022.

KB Ballentine's seventh collection, *Edge of the Echo*, was released May 2021 with Iris Press. Her earlier books can be found with Blue Light Press, Middle Creek Publishing, and Celtic Cat Publishing. When not tucked in a corner reading or writing, KB makes daily classroom appearances to her students. Learn more at www.kbballentine.com.

Tamara Baxter's collection of fiction, *Rock Big and Sing Loud*, won the Morehead State and Jesse Stuart Foundation's First Author's Award for Fiction. She is a recipient of the Harriette Arnow Award, the Sherwood Anderson Award, the Leslie Garrett Award in Fiction, and The Tennessee Mountain Writer's Award. Her work appears in *Mockingbird, The Cheat River Review, The Cold Mountain Review* and many others.

Barbara Costas Biggs lives and works in Appalachian southern Ohio. Her first collection of poems, *Broken On the Wheel*, was published by Cornerstone Press in 2021. Her work has been published by *Glass, Lost Balloon, Literary Mama, Ghost City Press, 8Poems*, and others. She has an MFA from Queens University of Charlotte and an MLIS from Kent State University.

Michele Binegar lives in Saint Marys, West Virginia and teaches Art and Graphic Design at Parkersburg High School. She earned dual Bachelor of Arts degrees in Graphic Design and Studio Art at Concord University in Athens, West Virginia. Her favorite mediums include painting, illustration and digital art.

Katlin Brock is a poet living in Harlan, Kentucky. She attended Lincoln Memorial University in Harrogate, Tennessee where she studied English literature. Her credits include *Jelly Bucket, Family Show Bear Circus, Fiction Southeast, Little Death Lit, HeartWood Literary*, three volumes of the *Anthology of Appalachian Writers* and the *NoSleep Podcast*.

Neva Bryan grew up in the mountain coalfields of Virginia. More than sixty of her short stories, poems, and essays appear in literary journals, online magazines, and anthologies. Her work has been published twice in the *Anthology of Appalachian Writers*. She has written several novels and a children's picture book.

Sarah Diamond Burroway earned her MFA in Nonfiction from Eastern Kentucky University's Bluegrass Writers Studio. Her thesis manuscript is an essay collection, *23: The Appalachian Foothills People, Place, and the Opioid Epidemic*. Her work has been published in *Still: The Journal, Sheila-Na-Gig, The Bitter Southerner, Women Speak*, and others.

Sam Campbell is a writer and teacher from Appalachia. She earned her English M.A. from East Tennessee State University, where she was the Editor-in-Chief of *The Mockingbird*. She currently serves *Arkansas International* as Managing Editor, and she is the fiction editor and co-founder of *Black Moon Magazine*. Her work appears in *MORIA, Poetry South*, and *Still: The Journal*.

Catherine Carter's most recent collection is *Larvae of the Nearest Stars* (LSU Press, 2019). Her poetry has appeared in *Best American Poetry, Orion, Poetry, Ecotone, RHINO*, and *Ploughshares*, among others. She lives with her husband in Cullowhee, North Carolina, and is a professor of English at Western Carolina University.

A storyteller with 30+ years' experience, **Omope Carter-Daboiku** has traveled internationally, sharing her experience as an Appalachian of mixed ancestry and Elder culture-keeper. She contributes to regional journals, supports Urban Appalachian communities, and facilitates capacity-building story circles and creative writing/theater projects for all ages.

Sheila Carter-Jones, author of *Three Birds Deep* and the chapbook *Crooked Star Dream Book* is a fellow of Cave Canem, Callaloo Creative Writing Workshop and a Walter Dakin Fellow of the Sewanee Writer's Conference. She holds an MFA from Carlow University and facilitates a writing workshop in the Madwoman Program.

Catherine Pritchard Childress teaches writing at Lees-McRae College. Her poems have appeared in *North American Review, Louisiana Literature, Connecticut Review, Appalachian Review*, and *Still: The Journal* among others, and have been anthologized in *The Southern Poetry Anthologies*, Volumes VI and VII. She is the author of the poetry collection *Other* (Finishing Line Press, 2015).

Jessica Cory was born and raised in Appalachian Ohio, where nearly all of her family still resides. She teaches in the English Studies department at Western Carolina University and is an English Ph.D. candidate at the University of North Carolina, Greensboro. She edited *Mountains Piled upon Mountains: Appalachian Nature Writing in the Anthropocene* (WVU Press, 2019).

Cecile Dixon is a retired ED nurse who, after a thirty-year sojourn to Ohio, has returned to her beloved Kentucky hills to write and raise goats. Cecile holds an MFA from Bluegrass Writers Studio. Her work has been published in *Dead Mule School of Southern Literature, Fried Chicken and Coffee, Pine Mountain Sand and Gravel, Still: The Journal, Women Speak, KY Herstory* and other anthologies.

Mitzi Dorton is the author of *Chief Corn Tassel* (Finishing Line Press). A multi-genre writer, her work has been featured in *Rattle, Rubbertop Review, The Dead Mule*, Women of Appalachia Project/*Women Speak, SEMO Press* and others. Her short story was featured in *Rise*, Northern Colorado Writers, 2020 Colorado Book Award in anthology.

Angie Dribben is an autistic artist and writer in the Appalachian region of Virginia. Her debut collection, *Everygirl*, finalist for the 2020 Broadkill Review Dogfish Head Prize, was released with Main Street Rag. Her most recent work can be found in *Los Angeles Review, Orion, Coffin Bell, Split Rock Review*, and others.

A native East Tennessean, **Sue Weaver Dunlap** lives deep in the Southern Appalachian Mountains near Walland, Tennessee. Her work has appeared in various journals. Her poetry books include *A Walk to the Spring House* (Iris Press, 2021), *Knead* (Main Street Rag, 2016), and *The Story Tender* (Finishing Line Press, 2014).

Ellis Elliott is a poet, writing group facilitator, and ballet teacher. She has a blended family with six grown sons. She has an M.F.A. from Queens University, is a contributing writer for the *Southern Review of Books*, and section editor for *The Dewdrop* contemplative journal.

Alyson Annette Eshelman's Appalachian heritage and faith have guided her creative outlet. Maintaining a home studio, she continues to create new works for exhibitions and accepts commissions for private and religious collections. Eshelman has participated extensively in solo, group, and juried exhibitions, receiving numerous awards for her work.

CJ Farnsworth is a poet residing in WV and a graduate of the Vermont College of Fine Arts MFA Program. Her poems have appeared or are forthcoming *in Rattle, Bluestone Review, Backbone Mountain Review, IMPOST: A Journal of Creative and Critical Work, Kenning, Kestrel, Poetry Quarterly*, and others. She is also a 2020 Pushcart Prize nominee.

Diana Ferguson, also known as DiFergi, was raised an Army brat, traveled the world and came to art late in life. At the age of 40, she graduated from college with a degree in Fine Art and set off on an intense journey of creating. Her work is whimsical, enigmatic and full of life and color. She has shown worldwide and fully intends to put down her paintbrush when she dies.

Lynette Ford's writing is rooted in storytelling and the narratives passed down in her Affrilachian family. Lyn is an award-winning writer, an Ohio teaching artist, a certified laughter yoga teacher, an international keynote speaker and workshop presenter, and a member of the National Association of Black Storytellers' Circle of Elders.

Jane Ann Fuller's *Half-Life* (Sheila-Na-Gig, Editions 2021) was a finalist in the 16th Annual National Indie Excellence Awards. A recipient of the James Boatwright III Prize (Shenandoah), Fuller hails from southeastern Ohio. Her poems appear in *Verse Daily, The American Journal of Poetry, BODY, Still: The Journal, PMS&G, On the Seawall*, and elsewhere.

Connie Jordan Green is the author of award-winning novels for young people, *The War at Home* and *Emmy*; poetry chapbooks, *Slow Children Playing* and

Regret Comes to Tea; and poetry collections, *Household Inventory*, winner of the Brick Road Poetry Award, and *Darwin's Breath*, Iris Press. She frequently leads writing workshops.

Kathy Guest, a paper artist who exhibits locally, regionally and internationally, has work in collections in the US, Poland, Bulgaria and Turkey. She is a member of the International Association of Hand Papermakers and Paper Artists (IAPMA), the world's leading organization for paper artists and a local artists' cooperative, Majestic Galleries.

Kari Gunter-Seymour is the poet laurate of Ohio, an Academy of American Poets Fellowship recipient and editor of ten anthologies. Her collections include *Alone in the House of my Heart* and *A Place So Deep Inside America It Can't be Seen* (winner 2020 Ohio Poet of the year Award). She has been featured in *World Literature Today, Poets.org* and *Verse Daily*. Find her at:
wwwkarigunterseymourpoet.com

Four-time Pushcart Prize nominee **Jennifer Hambrick** authored *In the High Weeds*, winner of the Stevens Manuscript Award from the National Federation of State Poetry Societies; *Joyride* (Red Moon Press), winner of the Marianne Bluger Book Award from Haiku Canada; and *Unscathed* (NightBallet Press). She is featured in *American Life in Poetry*.

Pauletta Hansel's newest poetry collection is *Heartbreak Tree*, an exploration of the intersection of gender and place in Appalachia. Her writing is featured in *Oxford American, Rattle*, and *Poetry Daily*, among others. Pauletta was Cincinnati's first Poet Laureate and is 2022 Writer-in-Residence for The Cincinnati and Hamilton County Public Library.

Ohio native, **Jessica Held**, first moved to Athens to earn a degree in painting and photography at Ohio University. After graduating and moving around the Midwest, years later she happily settled back in this wonderful community. Jessica creates functional artwork and teaches youth art camps and classes.

Melissa Helton's work has been published in *Shenandoah, Still: The Journal, Cutleaf, Anthology of Appalachian Writers*, and more. Her chapbooks include *Inertia: A Study* (2016) and *Hewn* (2021). She develops writing and agricultural programming for youth in southeast Kentucky where she writes and lives with her fella and two kids.

A native of upper East Tennessee, **Jane Hicks** is an award-winning poet, teacher, and quilter. Her poetry appears in both journals and numerous anthologies, including *Southern Poetry Anthology: Contemporary Appalachia* and *Southern Poetry Anthology: Tennessee*. Her first book, *Blood and Bone Remember*, won several awards. Her latest poetry book, *Driving with the Dead* (University Press of Kentucky, 2014) won the Appalachian Writers Association Poetry Book of the Year Award.

Leatha Kendrick's poems appear in journals and anthologies, including *Tar River Poetry, Southern Poetry Review, New Madrid Review, The Southern Poetry Anthology, Volume 3* and *What Comes Down to Us – Twenty-Five Contemporary Kentucky Poets.* Her fifth collection of poetry *is And Luckier* (Accents Publishing, 2020). She lives in Lexington, Kentucky.

Stephanie Kendrick works for the Athens County Board of Developmental Disabilities and has a Masters of Social Sciences. She is the author of *Places We Feel Warm* (Main Street Rag Publishing, 2021), and *In Any of These Towns* (Sheila-Na-Gig Editions 2020). Her poems have appeared in *Sheila-Na-Gig Online, Gyroscope Review* and elsewhere. Visit her website: stephthepoet.org.

Some of the journals that **Patsy Kisner's** poems have appeared in include *Appalachian Journal, Pine Mountain Sand & Gravel, Shelia-Na-Gig*, and *Spoon River Poetry Review.* Her poetry chapbook, *Inside the Horse's Eye*, and her poetry collection, *Last Days of an Old Dog*, were released from Finishing Line Press.

A native of Radford, Virginia, **Lisa Kwong** is AppalAsian, an Affrilachian Poet, and author of *Becoming AppalAsian* (Glass Lyre Press). Her poems have appeared in *A Literary Field Guide to Southern Appalachia, Still: The Journal*, and other publications. She teaches at Indiana University and Ivy Tech Community College.

Marlene L'Abbé is an artist from Montreal, Quebec, living many years in southeastern Ohio. It's here where she discovers through her painting the full expression of her life. Her art can be followed on Instagram, @waterspider3 and @marlene.labbe.art. Her tile art can be purchased from Etsy at tilemeastory.etsy.com

Jessica Manack lives with her family in Pittsburgh, Pennsylvania. Her poetry and essays have recently appeared in Five South, Maudlin House, and The Watershed Journal. She is a recipient of a 2022 Curious Creators Grant, which will enable her to keep telling the stories of this region.

Marie Manilla enjoys exploring issues of race, class, and gender in her work, which is often set in her home state of West Virginia. Her books include *The Patron Saint of Ugly; Shrapnel*; and *Still Life with Plums: Short Stories.* Marie recently served as Shepherd University's 2021 Appalachian Heritage Writer-in-Residence.

Karen Salyer McElmurray is the author of a memoir, *Surrendered Child: A Birth Mother's Journey*, winner of the AWP Award for Creative Nonfiction. She has published three novels—*Strange Birds in the Tree of Heaven, The Motel of the Stars*, and *Wanting Radiance* (University Press of Kentucky 2020).

Jonie McIntire, Poet Laureate of Lucas County, Ohio, has authored three chapbooks, including *Semidomesticated*, which won Red Flag Poetry's 2020 chapbook contest. She is poetry editor at *Of Rust and Glass* and is the Membership Chair at the Ohio Poetry Association. McIntire hosts Uncloistered Poetry from Toledo, Ohio. Learn about her at https://www.joniemcintire.net.

Wendy McVicker is at home in Athens, OH, where she is the 2020-2023 Poet Laureate. Her most recent chapbook is *Zero, a Door* (The Orchard Street Press, 2021). She loves collaborating and performing with other artists, and her involvement with *Women Speak* goes back to the beginning, in March 2009.

Barbara Marie Minney is a transgender woman, retired attorney, poet, speaker, and quiet activist. Barbara is the author of *If There's No Heaven*, the winner of the 2020 Poetry Is Life Book Award, and one of the Akron Beacon Journal's Best Northeast Ohio Books of 2020. Follow Barbara at www.barbaramarieminneypoetry.com.

Deni Naffziger lives in southeast Ohio. Her work has appeared in *New Ohio Review, Atticus Review, Pine Mountain Sand & Gravel, Pikeville Review, Pudding Magazine, Northern Appalachian Review*, and elsewhere. Her first book, *Desire to Stay*, was published in 2014. Her second collection, *Strange Bodies,* will be published by Shadelandhouse Modern Press in 2023.

Karen Whittington Nelson writes poetry and fiction from her home on a small, southeastern Ohio farm. Her work has been published in *I Thought I Heard A Cardinal Sing: Ohio's Appalachian Voices, Women Speak*, Volumes 2-7, *Sheila-Na-Gig Online, Northern Appalachia Review, the Anthology of Appalachian Writers, Gyroscope Review* and *Pudding Magazine.*

Valerie Nieman is the author of *In the Lonely Backwater* and four earlier novels, and books of short fiction and poetry. A graduate of West Virginia University and Queens University of Charlotte, she has held state and NEA fellowships. You can find her online sites at linktr.ee/ValNieman

Elaine Fowler Palencia, Champaign, IL, is the author of two short story collections, four pulp novels, four poetry chapbooks, a book of Civil War history, and a short monograph, *The Literary Heritage of Hindman Settlement School*. She is from Morehead, KY.

Frauke Palmer's studio is the out of doors. That's where she takes her pictures; that's where she finds her inspiration; that's where her ideas spring forth. Back home she sits in front of her computer and relives all those moments hiking through the wide-open landscape by creating a new world.

Lisa J. Parker is a native Virginian, a poet, musician, and photographer. Her book, *This Gone Place*, won the 2010 Weatherford Award and her work is widely published in literary journals and anthologies. Her book, *The Parting Glass*, won the 2021 Arthur Smith Prize and will be published by Madville Press in 2022.

Tina Parker is the author of three books of poetry, most recently *Lock Her Up* published by Accents Publishing in 2021. Tina grew up in Bristol, VA, and she is a long-time Kentucky resident. To learn more about her work, visit www.tina-parker.org or follow her on Instagram @tetched_poet.

Poet, playwright, essayist, and editor, **Linda Parsons** is the poetry editor for Madville Publishing and copy editor for Chapter 16, the literary website of Humanities Tennessee. Widely published, her fifth poetry collection is *Candescent* (Iris Press, 2019). Five of her plays have been produced by Flying Anvil Theatre in Knoxville, Tennessee.

Chrissie Anderson Peters hails from southwestern Virginia, but has lived in Bristol, Tennessee, since 2000. She lives with her husband and their four feline children. In addition to writing, her passions include 80's music. She has written three books. Read more about her and her writing at www.CAPWrites.com.

Rhonda Pettit, Ph.D., is the author of *Riding the Wave Train* and *The Global Lovers*, as well as literary criticism on the work of Dorothy Parker. She is a professor of English at the University of Cincinnati Blue Ash College, where she is editor of the *Blue Ash Review*..

Cat Pleska is an author, educator, and publisher. She holds an MFA in creative nonfiction writing. Her memoir, *Riding on Comets* was published by West Virginia University Press, 2015. Cat edited three anthologies and her essays have appeared in *Still: The Journal, Women Speak* Anthologies, and many others.

Susan Powers holds a BFA in Painting from Carnegie Mellon University with a minor in Creative Writing, and a MFA in painting from Pratt Institute. She is an Adjunct Lecturer in the department of Art at Carlow University. Visual perception, memory and the Appalachian environment influence her writing.

Bonnie Proudfoot lives on a ridgetop outside of Athens, Ohio. Her novel, *Goshen Road*, (Swallow Press, 2020), received the 2022 WCONA Book of the Year Award and was long-listed for the 2021 PEN/ Hemingway award for debut fiction. Her debut book of poems *Household Gods* (Sheila-Na-Gig) will arrive in 2022.

Rita Quillen's new novel, *Wayland*, a sequel to *Hiding Ezra*, (Iris Press in 2019), was the March, 2022 Bonus Book of the Month for the International Pulpwood Queens and Timber Kings Book Club. Her poetry collections include, *Some Notes You Hold*, (Madville Press, 2020) and *The Mad Farmer's Wife* (Texas Review Press, 2016), a finalist for the Weatherford Award. She lives in southwestern Virginia. www.ritasimsquillen.com.

Barbara Sabol's fourth collection, *Imagine a Town*, was awarded the 2019 Sheila-Na-Gig poetry manuscript prize. She is the editor of the poetry anthology, *Sharing This Delicate Bread*, forthcoming from Sheila-Na-Gig Editions. Her work has received Pushcart Prize and Touchstone Award nominations. Barbara's honors include an Individual Excellence Award from the Ohio Arts Council.

Teresa Sager's art is inspired by her surroundings: the trees, the hills, the way the light falls on them at certain times and the birdsongs right outside her window. She is madly in love with her Appalachian home and wants to bottle it up and put it in her paintings and poems.

Shei Sanchez's poetry has appeared in many fine places, including Women of Appalachia's *Women Speak* Volume 7, Woodhall Press's *Nonwhite and Woman, Main Street Rag, Still: The Journal, Sheila-Na-Gig*, and *One*. She lives with her partner on their farm by the Hocking River.

S. Renay Sanders' love affair with words began amidst a family of storytellers. Crafting stories lead her to poetry—story with a touch of rhythm, rhyme, and reflection. To this day, playing with words brings her joy. She hopes it brings the same to those with whom it is shared.

Susan Truxell Sauter's poems are published in many anthologies. Her poem, *Spring Rue*, was a part of the 2021 WVU Libraries Food Justice exhibit. She's at work on a poem for *Listening for Racial Understanding* organized by a Morgantown, WV church which will be displayed this year alongside other art and exhibited throughout West Virginia where she lives.

Roberta Schultz, author of four chapbooks, is a songwriter, teacher, and poet from Wilder, KY. She writes some of her songs on a mountain in North Carolina. She is co-founder of the Poet & Song House Concert Series with her Raison D'Etre trio mates. You can find out way more than you'd ever want to know about her at these websites: robertaschultz.com and raison3.com

West Virginia native **Carter Taylor Seaton** is the award-winning author of three novels, *Father's Troubles, amo, amas, amat...an unconventional love story*, and *The Other Morgans* and three non-fiction works: *Hippie Homesteaders, The Rebel in the Red Jeep*, and *We Were Legends in Our Own Minds*. She currently lives in Huntington, WV.

Susan Sheppard's poetry collection is titled *Glamoury* (Better Than Starbucks, 2021). She was a native West Virginian of Lenni-Lenape (Delaware), Shawnee and European ancestry and descended from some of West Virginia's earliest settlers.

Sylvia Bailey Shurbutt is Director of the Center for Appalachian Studies and Communities at Shepherd University and managing editor of the *Anthology of Appalachian Writers*. Her poetry and prose has appeared in a range of journals. She is author of books about travel and literature—her most recent *Silas House: Exploring an Appalachian Writer's Work* (UK Press, 2021) has been nominated for SAMLA's 2022 Book Award

Lacy Snapp is a poet and woodworker. Her first chapbook, *Shadows on Wood*, was published in 2021. She teaches American Literature at ETSU, runs her business, Luna's Woodcraft, and serves on the board of the Johnson City Poets Collective. She is currently an MFA candidate at Vermont College of Fine Arts.

Lois Spencer's short stories have appeared in *Women Speak, Anthology of Appalachian Writers, The Poorhouse Rag, Change Seven*, and *Northern Appalachian Review*. Her first short story collection, *To Tell the Truth*, will soon join her 2017 memoir, *In the Language of My Country*. Lois formerly taught English in Southeastern Ohio.

Renée Stewart is a singer, writer, and long-time performer. She sings lead for and is the primary lyricist for the Renée Stewart Band, who released their introductory EP, Stories, in Summer 2022. She lives in Pomeroy, Ohio with her thirteen-year-old son, Ross, and their black Labrador retriever, Ella Fitzgerald.

Elizabeth Tussey is a writer based in Pittsburgh, PA. She specializes in Appalachian studies, eco-poetics, and the collective memory of the Kent State shootings. Her work is featured in *Barn Owl Review, Postcolonial Text, I Thought I Heard a Cardinal Sing*, and the forthcoming collection, *Horrifying Children: Hauntology*.

E. J. Wade is a humanities educator and two-time Pushcart Award nominee. She is published in the *Anthology of Appalachian Writers*, and *The New Ohio Review*. Wade is pursuing a doctorate in Disability and Equity in Education at National Louis University and a Masters of Appalachian Studies at Shepherd University.

Jayne Moore Waldrop is the author of *Drowned Town* (University Press of Kentucky, 2021), *Pandemic Lent: A Season in Poems* (2021), and *Retracing My Steps* (2019), both from Finishing Line Press. She lives in Lexington, Kentucky.

Randi Ward is a poet, translator, lyricist, and photographer from Belleville, WV. She earned her MA from the University of the Faroe Islands and has twice won the American-Scandinavian Foundation's Nadia Christensen Prize. Her work has been featured on *Folk Radio UK, NPR*, and *PBS NewsHour*. For more information, visit randiward.com/about.

Donna Weems sings at Pattifest, Gardner Winter Festival, and the Osage street festival. She soloed for *Songs of Scott's Run* and is featured on the CD. She joined Al Anderson and friends, raising over $20,000 for Ugandan orphans. She was a cast member of the folk operetta, *The Hobo's Homecoming*.

Kory Wells is the author of *Sugar Fix*, poetry from Terrapin Books. Her writing has been featured on *The Slowdown* and appears in *The Strategic Poet* and elsewhere. A seventh generation Tennessean and former poet laureate of Murfreesboro, Tennessee, she mentors poets through the from-home creative writing program MTSU Write.

Born and raised in southern Ohio, **Mary Beth Whitley's** work is inspired by her memories of playing in the woods and across a dirt road in farm fields. Her dreamlike work combines photos and wax to reflect the beauty and importance of the Appalachian countryside.

Sherrell Wigal comes from generations of people living and working the land in Appalachia. With carefully chosen words, Sherrell encourages readers to move beyond their expectations. Her poems challenge and inspire. Sherrell's poetry has been published throughout the region and she conducts readings and workshops.

Dana Wildsmith's newest collection of poetry, *With Access to Tools*, is forthcoming from Madville Publishing in 2023. Wildsmith has served as Artist-in-Residence for Grand Canyon National Park and Everglades National Park and she is a Fellow of the Hambidge Center for Creative Arts and Sciences.

Kristine Williams lives in Athens, OH. She authored the chapbook, *Like an Empty House* (Finishing Line Press, 2021). She retired in 2017 from teaching communication courses at Hocking College and Ohio University. She lives with her husband and has two adult children who credit her with a love of both writing and teaching.

Marianne Worthington edits *Still: The Journal*, an online literary magazine she co-founded in 2009. Her work appears in *Oxford American, Sweet*, and *Chapter 16*, among other places. Her poetry collection, *The Girl Singer* (UP of KY, 2021) won the Weatherford Award. Marianne grew up in Knoxville, Tennessee, and lives in southeast Kentucky.

Karen Spears Zacharias is an author/journalist, and Gold Star daughter whose father was killed in Vietnam. Her work has been featured in the *New York Times, Washington Post, CNN, NPR, Huffington Post* and *Newsweek*. Karen's debut novel, *Mother of Rain*, was awarded the Weatherford for Best in Appalachian Fiction. Karen has served on the national advisory boards for the Vietnam Women's Memorial Fund and the Vietnam Memorial Wall Foundation. She volunteers with programs designed to help veterans and Gold Star families. KarenZach.com

Acknowledgments:

Atticus Review: "Bimbo and Smitty and Bags"
Balance of Five: "The Midwife"
Bloodroot: "The Robbery"
Dunkard Creek Exhibition: "Spirit of the Forest"
Gyroscope Review: "It Isn't Ever Delicate to Live"
Heartbreak Tree, (Madville): "Poem Written While Contemplating a
    Newly Dug Southern Kentucky Grave"
Lost Balloon: "Ex-Lover Speaks of Appalachia"
New Ohio Review: "Mysterious Ways"
OPEN: Journal of Arts and Letters: "Counting Backwards"
Pigeon Parade Quarterly: "Airing it Out"
Sheila-Na-Gig online: "Refashioned," "Raw Edge"
Some Notes You Hold (Madville 2020): "Some Notes You Hold," "Prayer
    for Birds and Sunrise," "Writers Block"
Still: The Journal: "Daughter-Mother," "I Surrender My Garden to Her,"
    "Letter for Home"
Sundress Publications: "Searching for Wonton Soup"

Sheila-Na-Gig Editions